AGILE
FOR BEGINNER'S

The Best Guide Ever On The Market To Learn AGILE Step By Step

©Jym Lawrence

Table of Contents

Introduction

I want to thank you and congratulate you for Downloading the book, "
AGILE FOR BEGINNER'S: The Best Guide Ever On The Market To Learn
AGILE Step By Step

In an age where flexibility and adaptability are buzzwords and traditional
is passé, Project Management techniques have been tweaked to give
optimum results and to reduce the end-to-end delivery cycle.

The goal of Project Management is to simply bring about beneficial
change or added value to meet unique goals and objectives and is
pertinently critical to the success of an enterprise.

If you are hearing the phrase "Agile Development" frequently around the
office, it's no surprise. More and more companies are turning to this
system that uses constant feedback and is adaptive to the changing tides
of a given project.

At its core, Agile Development includes software development
methodologies that use this flexible concept. Constant revision of
deadlines and expectations is key to the Agile process.

Rather than the traditional (or "old school") methods of managing a project, where what was done could not be undone, as it was discovered too late in the project, Agile takes a constant look at the scope and obstacles a software implementation has and bends to accommodate it in a reasonable manner. Planning, testing and integration throughout the project are necessary for a project's success.

Rather than the old school method where the project manager took the helm, ran the meetings and barked out orders, Agile allows teams to collaborate. Decisions are made as a group to ensure transparency and open communication.

Agile has been slow to be implemented in software system development worldwide, although certain components have been utilized for some time.

As more businesses see the dollars and time wasted in using a more rigid project management approach, more are turning to Agile methodologies and practices as a way to stay current, circumvent pitfalls and keep projects on time and under budget.

According to top industry experts, in order to be a good product manager, it is very important to have sufficient knowledge about the different methodologies of Agile Product Development. Product managers must keep a receptive mind about the agile product development methodologies to deliver innovative product design and development processes. Agile broadly constitutes a wide variety of methods for product development and management.

It is a set of software developing methods based on incremental and repetitive development, wherein solutions and needs evolve due to collaboration between cross functional and self-organizing teams.

Such a system fosters adaptive planning along with evolutionary development as well as delivery, a gradual and repetitive approach while encouraging flexible and rapid response to changes.

With every passing day, more and more companies are turning towards the different methodologies of Agile development. This is helping the business sector to be more responsive to the present day diverse market changes.

Not only is Agile helpful in the growth and expansion of a company but it is equally effective in creating great working relationships among all the members of a group. Agile increases shared accountability; keep projects more focused on the latest market and customer needs while improving the company's market positioning.

A number of product managers are scared in using and adapting the various methods of Agile product development and management. There could be millions of reasons for that- may be lack of in-depth knowledge about Agile, lack of interest and ability in working closely with product development, etc.

To bridge this gap of fear, product managers must comprehensively educate themselves about the Agile development and management methods. This BOOK is a perfect guide about Agile to get a clearer picture.

Individuals and interactions over processes and tools Working software over comprehensive documentation Customer collaboration over contract negotiation Responding to change over following a plan, that is, while there is value in the items on the right, we value the items on the left more.

Agile Project Management System is result-oriented and design is finalized before each task's execution phase as against the traditional model which relies on the stringent sequential approach. Unit test plans are written before coding in contrast to the unit test plans which are written after or during coding in the traditional methodology.

The masterstroke where Agile scores over bygone Project management methodology is the feedback-friendly environment rather than relying on standard tools & techniques. This makes Agile's way of working stand out as it imbibes a feeling of ease among all involved parties especially the project team.

A tested end-product is created at the conclusion of every phase which wins customer approval in the form of sign-offs motivating the team to achieve further based on quantifiable results.

As Agile's popularity rises, methodology adoption has become key discussion point of corporate meetings. The fact is whatever suits the need is best to use, not restricted to one type or using blended types.

Achieving success out of Agile is all about implementing it in the right way while gaining desired results from the same.

Chapter 1

The History Of Agile Project Management

Agile is not just a software development methodology but a way of working that helps deliver business value faster, cheaper and with less risk. If you are an IT professional within an IT department or organization, or if you are a business professional in any sector, Agile values, principles and practices can help you optimize your team, your deliverables and the related processes.

Agile started off as a software development and delivery methodology but over the last few years it has grown broader and scaled to the organization level. Organizations in all kinds of industry are finding that the Agile way of working is not just suitable for IT departments but for the organization as a whole and it is delivering tangible benefits in record time.

Agile is not a radical new way but rather an evolution of best practices and work philosophy that now has a definite shape and can be implemented to deliver substantial improvements. Agile Values are ideals that teams should pursue as a goal. Agile Principles are applications of the Agile Values or Ideals to a particular industry.

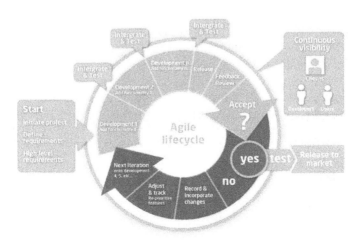

Value: Focus on business benefits and risk mitigation.

Collaboration: Focus on actively working together and leveraging collective knowledge.

Speed: Focus on time-boxed delivery and sustainable development.

Flexibility: Focus on adapting to business requirements and welcoming change.

Simplicity: Focus on keeping things simple.

Teamwork: Focus on creating empowered, self-adjusting teams.

Agile project management usually refers to a group of software development methodologies largely based on iterative development as requirements and solutions move through self-organizing multi-functional teams. The term Agile Project Management was coined in 2001 when the Agile Manifesto was created.

Agile project management usually aims to promote constant change and inspection; it is centered on team work and leadership as well as solo work that develops both customer needs and company goals.

The concept behind Agile project management can be found in modern approaches to analysis and management such as Six Sigma, soft system methodology and speech act theory.

Agile project management methods are sometimes discussed as being the other end of the spectrum from so called 'disciplined' or 'plan driven' methods of working.

This opinion is not strictly correct as it suggests that agile methods are not disciplined or planned. In reality agile methods work on a continuing improvement level with constant adaption in order to keep up to date.

Agile systems are constantly being compared to adaptive systems which are changing to solve real problems and issues so that when the needs of a particular project begin to change the adaptive team will also change to fit too. The downside to adaptive systems is that they will have difficulty predicting what will happen in the future.

On the other hand predictive methods tend to focus on planning the future in great detail. A predictive team can report exactly what features and tasks are planned for the entire length of the development process yet predictive teams have difficulty changing direction.

The main principles behind agile management systems are; priority of individual's actions over actions of tools and processes, customer collaboration over contact detail, the ability to respond to a challenge in a positive manner.

Working with Agile methodologies allows organizations to improve their product quality and also helps them to make sure those products and services can be brought to the market quickly and professionally.

When a company or organization begins to manage their projects using Agile project management methods, it is typical to see a marked increase in their growth and general expansion due to the high levels of productivity that are associated with Agile.

This project management method promotes and responds to change in an organic way, enabling a far more flexible approach to project development. Whilst this approach is very different to more traditional methods whereby the outcome of the project is planned thoroughly and the outcome is fixed, that does not mean that Agile project management has an undisciplined approach to working on a project.

The end result with Agile project management is always a little less predictable, in comparison with old methods, but this is not necessarily a disadvantage.

Because this method adapts to change in a positive way, responding to issues as they arise and resolving them, the result is always far more successful than the results obtained by a team who are simply ploughing forward blindly towards their end goal without ever seeming to consider a change of direction.

Agile project management encourages healthy and productive working relationships among colleagues who share accountability for the outcome of each project and work together to reach their goal. Regular team meetings play a key role in the success of this teamwork and make sure that everyone is focused and working effectively.

At these vital meetings, the team can be brought up to date on the progress that has already been made, before making plans together about the next stage of the process and preparing for its completion. Team members organize themselves without the need for a project manager and their shared skills mean they are able to carry out tasks effectively by assigning each task to the most suitable team member.

The ideal scenario when working on projects through Agile is for all parties working on the project to be housed under the same roof (i.e. one office) and in many ways this gives workers the opportunity to forge stronger relationships and certainly offers more convenience.

But this is not crucial and it can be quite straightforward to apply the principles of Agile with success in a broad range of other situations thanks to the fantastic array of technology we have at our fingertips to aid communication with one another.

The present state of the economy means that competition is tough and there is a great deal of emphasis on performance. Agile project management brings a lot to the table.

Through its forward thinking approach that is centered on teamwork and collaboration, Agile project management helps organizations to compete and keep up with the pace in a fast changing, diverse global market.

In terms of practicality and flexibility Agile delivers far more effectively than any of the more traditional methods and is therefore a highly useful option to explore.

Chapter 2

The Benefits Of Agile Development Methodology

BTo thoroughly comprehend the aspects involved in the agile application development, the preliminary requirement for the developer is to gain the clear idea about the technical architecture of the mobile application development.

This process involves lot of technical related challenges like in-depth knowledge of mobile programming language, consideration of contemporary strategic marketing principles, acute testing, app deployment and fierce app promotional activities thereafter.

Agile software development is one of the effective product development procedure, in which the entire process is breakdown into small individual blocks or components, which are technically programmed individually thereafter. This all chunks of task are then allocated to developers to independently accomplish it, as a part of the whole.

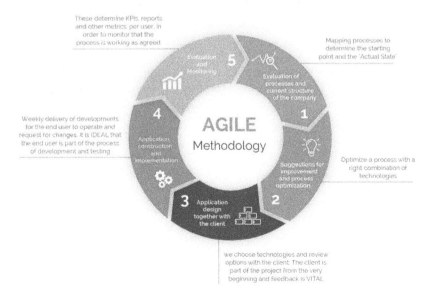

In this methodology, continuous communication among the involved entities of the project is quintessential, to keep the occurrence of any kind of flaws in the application, at bay. Here, we explore the list of benefits for choosing this methodology:

There are many advantages to agile development over the traditional models.

1) Agile development reduces the risk of client dissatisfaction

Since the stakeholders are involved in the process the entire time, the agile model reduces the risk that the product will not meet the needs of the client.

When the stakeholders are only involved in the requirements phase, they may not see that certain aspects of the design do not work or are irrelevant to their customer base. With everyone working together and continuously re-evaluating, the project is more likely to produce a useable product.

2) Allows for more change and adaptation

In the agile development method, the large, irreversible project elements are delayed until the last moment so as many changes as possible can be made to make sure the project is exactly right. Changes can be made after each increment; the designers are not stuck with one model.

Agile development is very adaptive to the changing needs of the client, the developers and the available technology. Because requirements can always change as new software is developed, these changes can be incorporated into the project instead of making the design obsolete before it ever goes to market.

3) Work can begin before all the requirements are known

Clients may not know everything they want in their finished product, but with agile development, they do not have to wait to get started working on the software.

They can start with a basic idea and because they are included throughout the development process, they can add requirements as they decide what they need and based on the work that has come first. Clients can continuously reprioritize so they have a usable product in a shorter amount of time

4) Increases likelihood that a project will reach the marketplace

A large amount of development projects never make it to the marketplace for various reasons including it was not what the client wanted, it is now obsolete, or it is not useful.

Using the agile development method, the chance that the product will go to the market is actually much higher because the chances that the client will approve of and find the product useful is higher. Also, the software developers can develop the highest priority designs first, allowing the product to be used immediately, even if it is not in its completed form.

5) Saves time and money

Stakeholders are involved in agile development throughout the process and everyone is working together, so the chance for miscommunication and incompatibility are smaller. This saves time by resulting in fewer mistakes and it saves money because the project is finished faster.

Once a client makes a decision on a requirement, they can see results quickly. The client will see results after each iteration and determine if the software meets their needs. Less time is wasted on features that are not going to be used.

6) Works well with distributed teams

Agile development is a method that can work when part of a project is outsourced, but is infinitely more successful if outsourced to a team in the same time zone. By having constant contact with the outsourced team, there will be fewer mistakes and miscommunications.

With nearshore outsourcing, the developers and outsourced team are working in the same time zone and language. People in other countries can easily keep in contact via email, phone and video conferencing. Agile requires more communication and more communication results in fewer mistakes and misunderstandings.

Shrinks your risk volume

The conventional waterfall methodology comes with a tons of drawbacks that have proved to decline the reliability rate of the developed application.

In terms of financial sense, agile is far more cost-effective compared to waterfall methodology. Parallel testing I.e. testing the programming line of code, itself during development aims to decrease the risk level, which is the core reason which distinguishes agile from other development methodologies.

High return on investment

Block wise development concepts of agile methodology, aids in completing and finishing the project within the stipulated time period.

Mobile applications which are developed through this approach have found to deliver higher ROI, due to their stringent technical feature capability. Here, all the involved business parties continuously coordinates with the project manager, to assure that everything is going as per planned.

Quality rich solution

In agile development process, development and testing are both performed in a simultaneous fashion, to ensure that the bugs are fired out. Agile is like interpreter, which translate each line of code at a time. This provides developers with the facility to modify the code, based on the number and type of features to be incorporated.

High level of customers satisfaction

When the product is developed through agile process, all its development related functional parameters are visible to the owner of the product. They continue to perform real-time analysis, and in the meantime if they find the development track irrelevant, necessary amends are immediately put into action.

Summing up

Agile development methodology is not only beneficial from the developers point of view, but also from the business perspective too. Many pitfalls in the project development like cost, time, feature scope etc. are seriously addressed, which can be the cause of hindrance for the development of an exquisite application.

Mobile application development companies across the globe have realized the potency of agile development approach, so as to launch a satisfactory quality product in the market.

Chapter 3

Principles And Guidelines Of Agile Methodology In Project Management

Agile Methodology is one of those methodologies which are widely used as tools of project management in software companies. It is based on incremental and iterative development.

The methodology involves cooperation between various cross functional teams in the organization, for obtaining the required resources and solutions for creating the ideal software and applications. The best part about agile methodology is that, it allows for continuous improvement in the development process.

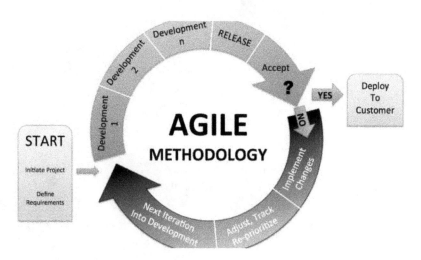

Principles

Here are the principles of agile methodology in project management:

1. Hierarchy - The decision to create a hierarchical structure within the development team depends a lot on the approach of the project

manager, in any case there is a secondary consequence not making this choice, if you insist on a hierarchical tree structure which is fragmented then you will get the chance to manage a very large number of programmers to work on different aspects of the project in parallel, if you insist on a complete lack of hierarchy there will be a development team, which will be very compact and motivated, but necessarily small in terms of number of programmers;

2. Pair programming - Programming in pairs, i.e., two programmers, two chairs, a desk, a computer, keyboard and mouse, one of the programmers writes, the other executes, while both choose the best construction solution. It is known to reduce the cost of the project, but there are practical examples that show how this practice can be unbearable for some programmers and counterproductive;

3. Refactoring - It is the complete rewriting of parts of the code which remain unchanged, the external appearance, the header syntax and other such details which can be re-written to derive a better result. It is one of the most common practices used in the management of software projects.

4. Improvement of knowledge - Founded with the advent of Object-Oriented Programming, is nothing but the realization of knowledge production that is done in a company as it produces code; this knowledge produced must not be lost and should be utilized in the production of new software in the future as well.

Objectives

The goal of agile methodology is full customer satisfaction and not only the fulfillment of a contract. The use of these methods also serves to reduce the cost of software development.

Guidelines

The guidelines, based on which this methodology is established, are the following:

Individuals and interactions are more important than processes and tools (i.e. relations and communication between the actors of a software project is the best resource of the project);

It is more important to have working software that records (must release new versions of software at frequent intervals, and you have to keep the code simple and technically advanced, reducing the documentation to a minimum);

We must collaborate with clients beyond the contract (direct collaboration offers the best results of the contractual relationships);

We must be prepared to respond to changes rather than join the project (so the development team should be allowed to suggest changes to the project at any time).

Practices

The individual files within this methodology are dozens and depend primarily on the needs of the company and approach of the project manager. The choice, however, must take into account the characteristics of each practice for the benefits they provide, and the consequences that entails.

For example, in Extreme Programming, it makes up for the absolute lack of any form of design and documentation with the close involvement of customers in the development and design partner.

The most common practices to choose from are similar to each other and can be grouped into categories:

Automation - If the goal of reading is to focus on programming methodologies without engaging in the side activities, then they can be eliminated or automated, and the second solution is better as elimination may result in many complications in the process of software development and may even alter the results of the project.

Basic Principles

The process of agile methodology applied in the field of project management (in software companies) has the following basic principles:

1. Close communication - According to Alistair Cockburn, probably the first theorist of lightweight methodologies, this is the only real aspect that makes nodal lightweight methodology.

For direct communication means the interpersonal communication between all stakeholders in the project, including client. This is to have a good requirements analysis and a fruitful collaboration between programmers, even in an environment of almost total absence of documentation;

2. Customer involvement - The involvement of the client is referred to herein individually as there are different degrees of involvement possible, such as Extreme Programming is total involvement, even to the customer participates in weekly meetings of the programmers, in other cases, the customer is involved in a first phase of the design and then no more, and in others the customer participates indirectly and is used in the test of the released version;

3. Design and documentation - Thinking that lightweight methodologies eliminate the design and documentation is an error, instead agile methodology makes it important for the project managers to create documents. Most project managers decide the amount of documents, and the kind of documents, needed to complete the software project.

4. Frequent deliveries - Making frequent releases of interim versions of the software allows the project managers to get more results at once: it provides the customer with "something to work with" and stops the occurrence of any delays in the delivery of the complete design, by making sure that the customer gets the product (software) on time.

In this process, the project manager can obtain more precise information on the customer requirements that they would probably not be able to express without having a trial version of the software, which will help them to understand its shortcomings.

Chapter 4

Intermediate Processes Involved In Agile Project Management

Agile Development process is a collection of incremental and iterative methodologies used to develop highly scalable, modular and robust software applications. One of the general misconceptions about agile process is that there is absolutely no requirement for agile project management.

Further, some people perceive that agile projects run on their own. In reality, the decreased focus on detailed plans result in this perception. Its impact is that a project manager in an organization, which was involved in the process of agile project management, was shifted to another area since the organization obviates the need for managing people.

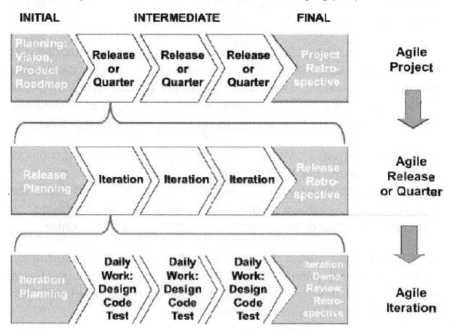

The success or failure of any project depends on the extent and adherence of project management processes from planning to handover of the project. In the absence of proper project management processes, a project may go for a toss missing deadlines, becoming buggy and escalating the cost.

In agile development, the process of project management goes a few steps ahead by using historical data and re-engineered components along the skills acquired due to high-level of maturity in software programming that strictly follows project management techniques.

There are various intermediate processes involved in Agile Project Management:

The project is owned by the product vendor whose activity lies in managing the vision of the project. Accordingly, the product vendor establishes, promotes and communicates the product version. The product owner initiates the process of funding for the project by way of developing initial release plans and the basic product backlog.

The project is handled by the product vendor who manages the activity of ROI (Return on Investment). Further, the product owner handles a set of responsibilities that include monitoring the project as-is its ROI goals and investment vision.

Also, the product vendor takes upon himself to update the product backlog and prioritize to ensure that highly valued functionality is produced first and built upon. In addition to it, the product vendor evaluates success against prices.

The project is led by an individual who manages the development iteration. As part of this iteration, the project lead builds the team and sets the top priority features corresponding to the product backlog. Jointly, the team magnifies product backlog items into more clear tasks on a sprint backlog and succeeds in completing assigned tasks.

Scrum Methodology

In Scrum methodology, the Scrum Master assumes the responsibility of achieving success by ensuring the project and management culture are optimized for reaching the ROI goals of the project.

Extreme Programming

Extreme Programming is a software development methodology, which is aimed at improving the quality of software and enhancing responsiveness to the varying requirements of customers.

As a part of agile software development, it facilitates frequent releases in short growth cycles to enable enhanced productivity and presenting checkpoints where new customer needs can be adopted. It ensures successful results since it focuses on customer satisfaction. It develops a software project in five important ways - communication, effortlessness, response, respect and courage.

Waterfall Method

The Waterfall approach is a sequential design process employed in software development. It takes its birth in the standard workflow procedure in the construction and manufacturing sector.

Agile and Waterfall are two separate approaches to software development that are used in project management. Both have their respective advantages and disadvantages.

The choice of these methods depends on different project-centric factors. In the case of Waterfall approach, the benefit lies in the division of the project into tight partitions thereby decreasing the reliance on individuals.

Chapter 5

Common Agile Misconceptions

Agile Development is a powerful approach, particularly in IT. It can help produce quality products in a quick, efficient manner. However persuading people to be "Agile" usually involves overcoming a number of common misconceptions.

"Agile development is not disciplined"	"Agile development is just another fad / hype"	"Agile means teams cannot be controlled by management"
"Agile teams do not plan"	"Agile means you never have to write documentation"	"Agile works only for small projects; it does not scale"
"Agile development is not predictable"	"Agile means I can change my mind whenever I want to"	"Agile teams do not work hard, they just play foosball"

1) We can't use Agile with our business model.

Sure you can. If you have tasks, then you can use Agile. Agile has been implemented in very complex business environments, including Banking and Finance, Healthcare, Insurance, Payment Processing and many more. Agile offers a great deal of transparency and accountability, which is often why people in some environments are hesitant to make the move to Agile.

2) There were instances when teams would try to manipulate Agile to handle an outdated process that was extremely inefficient and time-

consuming. Agile is about being efficient and effective, so that process should not impede the end goal of delivering the working software or product. For instance, I have worked on projects in which there were 20+ steps to completing a Story (over three 3-week Iterations/Sprints).

What we have to remember is that this creates 20 potential points of failure and for every individual involved in the process, that 20 gets multiplied by the number of individuals touching the process.Even in those industries where there is extensive governance and bureaucracy, 5 steps can create a tremendous bottleneck in the process, which will negate any benefits that could be attained by Agile.

This is why I strongly urge teams to refactor the process to the methodology; don't contort the methodology to fit the process.

If there is a cumbersome process, this may be a very strong case for doing "Value Stream Mapping", to review the process for effectiveness. Personally, I recommend this occurring regularly since, over time, some processes become outdated or burdened with unnecessary steps due to politics and hidden agendas.

3) When it comes to making a project fail, if you mix in enough process and politics, alone, it will certainly fail. If it does succeed, it will cost 4 to 5 times more than originally planned.

Why don't Agile and Waterfall work well together? Wouldn't it be like getting the best of both worlds? Agile and Waterfall/ SDLC are polar opposites, and when you introduce polar opposites, the sum gain is 0.

Waterfall and Agile mixed together do not work and it will be a constant tug of war, in which productivity will suffer. Waterfall is very process and procedure-heavy, whereas Agile is very process and procedure-light. This is why I have found that Business / System Analysts and Quality Assurance professionals tend to dislike Agile. The cornerstone of their work is based on process and procedure.

In considering all the above, there is a recent craze in Water-gile/ SCRUM-afall, which involves using the terminology of Agile and SCRUM, while still following the processes surrounding Waterfall.

These projects have a tendency to stall, because they are still process-heavy. For instance, many environments try to do the following in the name of Agile: Iteration/Sprint 1 - Analysis, Iteration/Sprint 2 - Development, Iteration/Sprint 3 - Quality Assurance.

While on rare occasions there may be a need to follow this process, in the end, a User Story has taken 3 Sprints/Iterations to complete, which can take somewhere in the neighborhood of 6 to 9 weeks. This allows almost no time for course correction, if the team is going down the wrong path.

When it comes to Agile, there are steps to being successful. Our goal is always to help teams reach that success.

4) "We don't need to plan on Agile projects." Yes you do! Coordinating work so that it can finish within short sprints needs careful planning. Tools like burn down charts help monitor whether we are on track by providing estimates of how much work remains

5.) "Agile is a sloppy, ill-disciplined way of developing." I would say the reverse is true. Agile engineering practices such as test driven development, automated builds and continuous integration create a very focused, transparent and efficient way of building a product.

6.) "Agile projects deliver sooner" This could be true, especially if we are used to creating large, superfluous artifacts like requirements documents. It's also certainly true that in Agile we are trying to deliver something sooner than a more traditional waterfall method.

However we may need to go through a number of iterations of delivering interim deliverables and getting feedback Keeping the client involved in these iterations should produce a higher quality product.

7.) "Agile is easier for the client." Actually in some ways it is harder, as the client needs to be more heavily involved in developing requirements. Unless the benefits are properly explained (i.e. better end products) this can lead to irritated customers.

8.) "Agile will be too chaotic to track progress." Actually Agile is completely transparent. For example it is very easy to know what each developer is doing via the daily Scrums and the burn down charts. It is also simple to know quickly whether the system works by building it automatically and running automated tests against it.

9.) "We don't need testers in Agile Development." One of the features of an Agile approach is to blur the distinction between testing and developing. For example, developers write unit tests focused on the structure of the code.

It is still important that testers carry out business-focused tests, non-functional tests such as performance and load testing, and put themselves in the mind of a user by doing manual tests. See the excellent Agile Testing by Lisa Crispin for a full discussion on the testers role in Agile.

10.) "We don't need business analysts in Agile Development." Wrong. Because clients will be more involved in Agile Development, the skill of helping them articulate their needs and explaining and selling to them why they need to be more heavily involved is more important than ever.

11.) "You just need a Scrum Master Certification to implement Agile." Well it certainly helps, but Scrum only tells half the Agile story. It focuses on management practices such as using sprints, product backlogs and allocating different roles to stakeholders.

What it doesn't look at are the engineering practices such as test driven development, automate builds and continuous integration. To get an understanding of these you could look at Extreme Programming by Kent Beck.

12.) "Scrum teams are never disturbed once they start a sprint." Keeping the team away from interruptions so they stay focused is an important part of the managing with Scrums. However common sense should always prevail over blindly sticking to a process - there are times when Scrum teams need to be redirected during a sprint.

13.) "Agile is always the best approach" For large project with many team members, one final end deliverable and a low risk of misunderstanding what the client needs, a more traditional Waterfall approach might be more applicable.

Chapter 6

Cost Reduction With Agile Methodology

While there are many advantages of agile, including more control on the part of the product owner and less risk of the product not going to market, the reduction in the actual cost of development is one of the most important advantages. Agile development is a strategy of software development in which the development process occurs though short increments. The phases of the development process occur continuously in iterative cycles, with each team member and the product owner sharing in the responsibility for producing "potentially shippable" software at the end of each iteration or "sprint".

The team meets after each increment to discuss what has occurred, re-evaluate requirements and determine priorities. This allows for greater transparency between clients and programmers and clients have greater influence in what is being designed to ensure the product is what they want

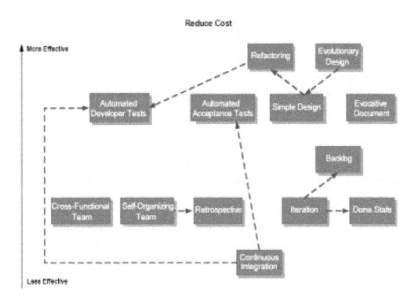

This is a departure from the traditional "waterfall" method, which typically involves the product owners during the requirements phase; then the development team takes over and develops the application.

In agile methodology, there is no upfront requirements document detailing all the work that will be done on the project because it changes constantly. Initially, software development companies may have difficulty budgeting for the project when so many things are unknown at the beginning.

However, the development team works with user stories which are short descriptions of application functionality from the perspective of the user. A collection of user requirements are stored in the product backlog, to be developed as the project continues.

The development team assigns each user story an estimation of the amount of time and effort the team will need to put forth to complete. Once the most important user stories have been identified, the project manager can determine a budget to present to the product owner. Of course, with agile methodology, there are bound to be changes, but it is possible to determine a budget up front that is a good estimation of production costs.

The main way agile methodology can reduce costs in software development is by reducing the amount of time it takes to bring a useable product to market. Agile methodology focuses on developing the most important aspects of the project first. If an aspect of the system does not work, it will become evident early in the process and there will be little time wasted on something that will not work.

Also, if the system is not exactly what the product owner or user had in mind, it can be altered immediately. The development team does not waste time developing aspects that will get little or no use by the user.

The project is continuously tested to ensure it is running correctly. A useable function of the system is completed after each iteration. Each meeting at the end of an iteration provides an opportunity to make sure the system is working and contributing toward a finished product. The team is not waiting until the end to see if the program runs correctly, resulting in costly and time-consuming changes.

Agile is about collaboration and communication is key. Less time is spent dealing with miscommunication because the team meets often. All members of the team meet so everyone agrees and is made aware of what is being developed. The product owner is included in all meetings to ensure he or she is getting exactly what is needed.

Less cost is associated with overhead in agile methodology. Management and administration occur within the team and extra staff is not required, for example, to write the requirements document at the beginning as with the waterfall method. Staff is not needed to schedule meetings and track down members of the team because everyone is aware that meetings happen regularly and are required.

Agile is an effective method for working with distributed teams. Outsourcing or nearshoring may be instituted to reduce costs, and utilizing agile will ensure multiple teams work well together by reducing miscommunication and catching errors quickly.

Agile methodology can reduce costs for a software development company. However, it is important to have an end point so the budget can accurately reflect what the project can entail.

When there is no upfront requirements document, the team could continuously make changes to the system, extending the project indefinitely. Once a company becomes comfortable with the agile methodology, it will begin to see reductions in costs.

Chapter 7

Agile Programming Scrum Armed With An Agile Manifesto

The overall goal of this chapter is to specifically identify approaches that worked well in software development and concurrently to show what avenues should be avoided. Interestingly, these four do's and don'ts directly conflict one another as presumably they must. So let's look briefly at each of the four Agile manifesto points.

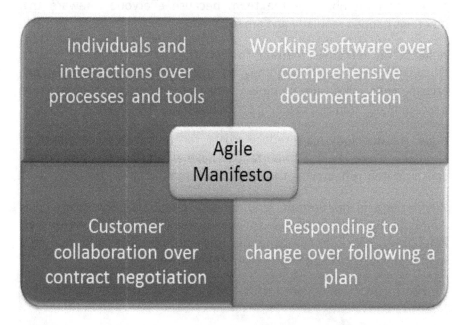

1 - 'Individuals and Interactions over Processes and Tools'. Developing software is about forging into new ground. Processes and tools are wheels that have already been invented and fires that have already burned. Individuals interacting are always into new ground or they would just be boring each other to tears. New wheels don't need reinventing but individuals interacting can uncover new things that can burn brighter.

2 - 'Working Software over Comprehensive Documentation'. An example to illustrate this concept this that comes to mind is that you are reading a 400 page manual on how to construct a working windmill but when you get to the final page it says - Warning - These instructions are hypothetical because we've never actually built a windmill using these plans. This is a bit of a no-brainer. A mousetrap has to catch mice before the press releases are on the presses.

3 - 'Customer Collaboration over Contract Negotiation'. Think of some of the times you've called a support line for some product or service you've been having some problems with. Would you rather be talking to someone who wants to solve your problem or someone explaining to you why the terms of service means he doesn't actually have to help you at all? Those 14 Agile manifesto developers were right bang on the money here.

4 - 'Respond to Change over Following a Plan'. The brilliant military strategist Sun Zsu wrote something in his book - the art of war - that certainly applies here. 'A tactical plan is only effective until first contact with the enemy.'

Manifesto for Agile Software Development

What's good about agile software development - it brings flexibility and convenience. What's bad about it - the agile approach can be misused and misunderstood as something that lacks planning, something that brings an incomplete software product which always requires a bunch of updates after it's rolled out to the market. But it's not necessarily this way.

The Agile Manifesto proclaims the main principles of agile development. Meanwhile, methodologies are adopted to individually suit each development company. Agile approach means good for you, software owner, if the company you've chosen follows these values and work principles.

Agile development consists of iterations. This means, the software owner receives a viable piece of software at the end of each iteration.

First it's the design of the future product; then is launched the development, where the product receives new features and gets tested, iteration by iteration.

Besides, the software owner can track the progress of development by receiving timely reports. Furthermore, this allows the owner to shape the picture of the app by giving feedback and altering requirements.

Requirements tend to change, that's for sure; and these unexpected changes may cause certain delays and overpays. Experience shows that initial requirements are always altered at will of the software owner.

These requirements may vary from insignificant ones to those which require rewriting quite a bulk of code. Agile method presupposes better adaptation to these changes. Changes may touch the industrial progress, and here agile is also a winner, keeping track of the ever improving tech and software.

Another characteristic of agile development is communication between the development contractor and the software owner. Very often it happens so that software development is not one-time service, but a real long-term partnership, fruitful for both parties.

The software owner is in control of the process, and communication plays a huge role of making parties better understand each other. As a result, it takes less time for the project to be finished, and the software owner receives exactly what he/she wants.

Some criticize agile approach as the one that rolls out an unfinished product to the market, then brings a bunch of updates to make something attractive out of it. This statement is a bit misleading. The more complex the project is, the more problems it may face, by any way of development.

Of course, everything depends on the quality and expertise of the company. But the simple rule is, software has to get feedback, and measures (updates) must be taken anyway, it just needs to be maintained relevant. That's how it gets better and better. The software will never be perfect to the eyes of the owner. But it can be directed towards perfection.

Haste might make waste, but speed by agile development doesn't. Speed is an advantage of quick releases and updates - the software owner becomes more agile on the market.

And there is always a business decision, an unexpected feature that the owner wants to incorporate into a flexible code. The most important decisions aren't always made at the beginning of the project, you can't predict everything.

What's valued within agile companies, is friendly, engaging atmosphere, necessary conditions, and motivation. Motivation of employees instead of strictness - this may cause accusations of lack of discipline. But that isn't like letting things fall where they may.

Nobody canceled order and elaborated work process, and the programmers' hourly achievements in creating the product are as transparent as can be; the software owner always knows what he/she pays for. There are a lot of tools to keep relations transparent, even for the most doubting and demanding software owners.

Agile can be interpreted in different ways by different companies. Agile development does not mean absence of documentation or poor quality. Self-organization and motivation does not mean absence of order and discipline. There's no magic in it, agile simply works. Planning is highly important.

Agile makes your software better if you choose the company that truly gets into the simple philosophy of agile development - providing the software owner and end users with a working result, and maintaining support thereafter.

Chapter 8

Agile Development In A Globally Distributed Team

Agile is considered to be a lightweight methodology. Unlike more structured traditional development methods it is claim for flexibility even in situation where changing or ambiguous projects requirements seem to be the norm.

Agile methodology over the years has become an integral part of organization's software development process, allowing organization to be nimble and flexible in bringing in their product and services in the market.

For the past few years organizations have turn up into agile methodologies and consider it as the breath of fresh air for the software development process. Agile offers a flexible and practical approach to development that the traditional methods can't deliver.

Organizations are implementing agile development to varying degrees, to increase speed to market their product, increase productivity, growth strategy, improve operation effectiveness processes, improve product quality etc.

Even in the case of distributed teams agile methodology has the potential to achieve similar objectives despite the fact that the very idea of physically distributing teams seems to conflict with agile communication practices.

Ideally in an agile environment, developers, Product Owner or business partners are in close proximity and sit under one roof.

This co-location typically facilitates several benefits of Agile: improve efficiency, frequent communication and feedback, continuous collaboration opportunity, a sense of ownership, foster closer working relationship and team can learn from other team practices.

However there are situations when managers have to manage distributed team comprised of both onshore and offshore resources. These distributed agile teams often have unique challenges that the agile process doesn't address. But given proper tools to work an organization can curtail the major bottlenecks of distributed teams.

Agile methodology can be equally effective even in the case of distributed teams given the teams are provided with adequate tools to maximize communication across geographically distributed environments.

Distributed agile development makes it possible to tap into new global markets and more importantly can complete a project in a faster rate if teams in different time zones continuously work on a particular project that potentially reduces costs.

In an ideal agile environment tools are not consider the primary focus of agile teams, but if selected properly they can certainly make teams more effective and efficient.

Distributed agile teams may not be able to rely on the usual agile methods of face-to face team meetings, sticky notes, task boards, or burndown charts on a wall for tacking an updating their project work status.

What is essential for the distributed teams are a robust system that can help the team to provide certain benefits provided they are flexible and do not hinder a team's natural workflow: Information sharing, level of documentation, co-ordination between multiple teams, communication channels, status tracking and reporting, frequency of meetings.

If the team is distributed, the organization should make conscious efforts to curtail as much of the lost communication bandwidth with augmented processes and practices:

Bringing teams together via video conferencing as often as possible, especially during planning and critical points during projects

Use of Digital wall so that each team members have updated work flow all the time

Team manger should have a clear mandate and should ensure that each team members stay on track with communication practices

Provide distributed teams with tools that will help them fulfill these user stories

Favor integrated systems that offer full traceability from specification design through development and testing

Integrated wiki linked to tasks and stories to store notes from various design meetings and impromptu conversions

In current economic market with so much pressure on performance, revenue generation agile methodology can give a competitive advantage at any given time. Agile methodology success is based on team work.

The thinking behind agile is collaboration and working together as a team. Most traditional models are very rigid and don't enable changes - thus relatively less flexible than the Agile model. Because of this nimble approach, Agile has a comprehensive response to most of the challenges organizations' face in a rapidly changing, competitive global market.

Chapter 9

Traditional Testing Vs Agile Testing

In this chapter. We'll take a brief look into the worlds of Traditional vs Agile testing.

Testers working on Traditional teams

Traditionally testers are only involved right at the end of the SDLC/PDLC value chain. They had no inputs into the writing of the requirements. During development they didn't have the opportunity to quickly pick up 'issues' and have them attended to by the team.

In traditional teams testers morph into some gatekeeping role, always protecting the near-stable release. Remember we are behind schedule as the development effort took longer than expected!

Any changes to the software requirements were scheduled for the next release. Traditional teams are expected to deliver the project scope in its entirety. An all or nothing approach. If all features aren't ready on the 'go-live' date the release is usually postponed.

Team members rarely have a say in which features are included in the release and developers tend to specialize in one specific area of the codebase. Collaboration is usually replaced with a sense of competitiveness. As you can see this is not what we are after in any method.

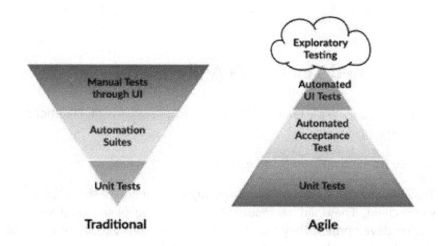

Traditional   Agile

Testers working on Agile teams

Moving from traditional- to Agile testing has one facing short bursts of productivity (Sprints) repeated until the product is 'done'. Within the boundaries of these Sprints, the entire PDLC/SDLC activity is completed, from analysis, design and coding to testing and post release support, all happening in one team, every day.

Agile teams work closely with business and detailed understanding of business problem areas that require solving. The team may have inputs into prioritizing the work as they can share pertinent information about the technical enablers that need to be in place for certain functionality to work.

As Agile methods are incremental, the Agile tester tests the user stories or requirements as they are deployed to the test environment. Fundamentally different to traditional methods, in Agile the whole team delivers a piece of functionality every day or so.

Programmers never get ahead of testers, as within the confines of the Sprint all team members are required to assist with testing.

"In Agile, quality is a team sport!"

In Agile, the whole team is responsible for quality whereas in traditional methods it was only testers that were accountable for software quality.

Agile team members start thinking about test cases the moment the customer makes known the requirements. Developers code the tests before the actual coding starts and test analysts extend the testing harnesses, all before the code has been completed that implement the user story.

Using agile project management techniques is not a million miles away from traditional methods. You still do the same work and arrive at the same end goal, but with the agile method work tends to be faster, more productive and risks tend to be diminished. Here's why.

Traditional project management

This method, also known as the waterfall method, is the most widely used form of PM worldwide. It typically involves six key steps from start to finish:

1. Requirements

2. Design

3. Development

4. Integration

5. Testing

6. Deployment

Each one stage is completed before the whole team moves onto the next stage, making this sequential method seem like something of a waterfall cascade, hence the name. Not all projects include all stages, and some may include a few more, but in essence this is the formation of waterfall PM.

Traditional PM is widely accepted as being valuable for smaller, well designed projects, but can sometimes struggle when dealing with larger and less well defined situations. It is designed for use in construction and manufacturing industries, where later changes are impossible or not cost effective, meaning everything needs to be done in a certain order.

Agile PM

The agile method differs in that everything can take place in any order, and is not necessarily sequentially completed. The method relies on human interaction management, and works on the project as a set of small tasks which are defined and completed as the demand arises. Large projects can be simply broken down into smaller components, known as 'sprints', and tackled for a short space of time until complete.

In agile, the design, testing, integration and development are all undertaken during each sprint, which makes the likelihood of errors being built into the final project much less.

This means there may be major changes made throughout the lifespan of the project, and the final product might not be exactly what was envisaged at the start. It will, if done right, be relevant, useful and flawless.

Which is best?

The most suitable method for managing your project is something you will need to decide for yourself. It will largely depend on the type of project you are delivering, as well as the scale.

Projects involving creative industries or software development benefit much more naturally from agile than those involved in creating physical products, as they allow for changes to be made even at very late stages in the project delivery.

Consider how stable the requirements of the project are. Projects that are likely to undergo changes to the brief or the requirements will respond much better to an agile project management framework, whereas those with well-defined business requirements and where certain stages need to be completed before moving on are more suited to traditional PM.

Chapter 10

How To Maximize The Value Of Functional Testing In An Agile Environment

Quality has always been a great factor for any software products or applications and with customers becoming more tech savvy and sophisticated, the market has become very competitive leaving no change for errors or bugs.

Based on the requirements of the projects and the technology used to develop the solutions, developers adopt the agile methodology so that the changes can be easily implemented while developing the application.

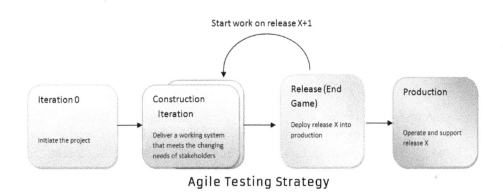

Agile Testing Strategy

But while developing, it is also important to continuously test the project, so that there are no bugs in the later phase of the development, which may be very difficult to change and even costly.

In an agile environment, the role of a software tester goes simply beyond "just testing" and logging errors and it is more working with the development team closely and with the product owner. The testers work with everyone to improve the quality of the product as early as possible.

How to maximize the value of good testing practice in the Agile environment:

Agile is all about maintaining high quality and focusing on the customers. Research has stated that testing plays a significant role to play in an agile environment and it can actually strengthen the output of the process. To maximize the value of this testing discipline it is suggested that:

A test driven approach is to be adopted as an effective practice to improve the quality of the product and eliminate duplication.

The role of a tester becomes richer and influential when they work together in a process where the developers, users and the testers themselves can bring their particular expertise.

A proper test strategy and planning should be done and the plans have to be flexible and adaptable to the new information that is produced at iteration.

Functional testing reduces the inefficient processes and helps to rectify them and also support the flexible agile principle.

How functional testing helps:

Leaving aside the skill levels of the team members, the quality of the project is also determined by the software processes that has produced it. Testing plays a great role in it and functional testing helps to test the interface between the users on one side and the rest of the system on the other side.

It requires a planned approach that includes the test execution and planning as well as the analysis that ensure maximum test coverage, reusability and consistency of testing efforts.

The QA testers capture the requirements and check the application to instill confidence in the developers as well as the users that the project meets the requirements stated and confirms further that the product is ready for production release.

Managing functional testing in the Agile environment:

Functional testing services actually start with gathering the testing requirements and then continue with the designing and developing tests, execute the test cases and analyses the product defects.

Arrange for a product presentation from the business team, as this will help to reduce the communication gap between what the team is actually developing and the market requirements. In the agile environment, the key principle is to demonstrate each iteration, so that it ensures that the requirements are clearly understood and implemented.

Functional testers should always collaborate closely with the developers throughout the testing life cycle and gather the test requirements all the way till the release of the product.

A traceability matrix should be prepared that documents the links between the requirements and the features, test cases and the requirements and between the test cases and the issues.

Maintain traceability matrices for any essential requirement changes, modifications related to test cases, test plans and traceability matrices at both the levels.

Reduced learning curve for each feature as the traceability matrices are easy and quick to go through.

Role of the functional tester:

The nature of a tester's role changes in any interactive project and they are no longer the only advocates of quality. So, for testers this is great news and the entire team has to adapt to the new context when they choose to work in an agile environment. Agile in the true sense means fast paced and changing and this means that the roles and responsibilities are also likely to flex and change quickly.

The testers have to be technically aware of what they are exactly testing and its impact on the entire project. An effective agile tester should know how to write and interpret code as well as understand how to test any component functionally to an acceptable level of coverage.

The Agile environment is adopted by most companies for efficient and rapid delivery of high quality software. Functional testers play a major role in quality assurance and it is only a flexible and adaptable approach that can help to maintain the standards of the product.

Chapter 11

Issue Management And Tracking With Agile Project Management Tools

Issue management with agile project management tools will vary, depending upon an organization's software development environment.

Agile development teams handling smaller, less complex development projects don't typically deal with a lot of bugs. Therefore, they may decide to stop using a dedicated bug tracking tool and rely entirely upon their agile project tool for managing issues.

Why have two lists of things to do?

By keeping everything in one force-ranked backlog in the agile project management tool, it is often easier for the product owner to make priorities clear to the team, and it will give team members better visibility into all issues as they arise.

In addition, the team will still be able to see the origin of every issue, who is handling that issue, what changes have been made, and when the issue is closed or completed.

The situation may be completely different for development teams that manage large, complex development projects and that log hundreds of bug reports a week.

Using an agile project management tool alone for tracking issues will not work. Take a video game company, for example, that may get 200 bug reports every week for one version of a product they are developing.

Many of the bug reports they receive are likely duplicate issues. By integrating their agile project management tool with a bug tracking system, they will be able to triage and consolidate issues before they wind up in the agile project management tool's product backlog.

The real benefit of combining an agile project management tool and a bug tracking system is that it becomes a one-stop shop for tracking all issues, and teams can leverage the best features of both systems.

Agile software tools enable teams to manage issues at a project level and provide reports and views such as burndown charts and workload balancing that do not typically exist in a bug tracking platform.

The bug tracking system, on the other hand, will allow agile teams to manage issues at a very detailed ticket level, customize workflow, and centralize issue information in the platform's repository.

Agile development teams that work in large distributed or highly regulated development environments will need to go one step further. They will likely need to integrate their agile tool with a more powerful platform such as an application lifecycle management (ALM) platform.

• • • Key Components of Agile Risk Management Target State

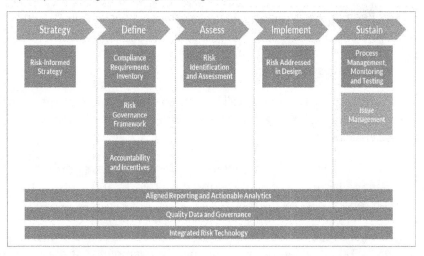

Key capabilities of an ALM platform include the ability to handle issue tracking at a very detailed level, and to provide capabilities for change management, custom workflow, source code management, task management, testing, lab management, collaboration, and reporting and analytics.

Best-of-breed ALM platforms also have integrated tracking capabilities that enable "traceability"-- the ability to easily associate, or link together, objects also referred to as "artifacts," within the system. Association simplifies knowledge sharing and provides traceability of an object throughout its lifecycle. So for example if we think of a customer reported issue" as the object:

1. The issue is entered into the system,

2. The issue can be linked to

• The original report describing the bug or feature request

• The source code generated to resolve the issue

• The release containing the fix

• Emails and discussions around the issue

• Any other artifacts that need to be associated with that issue

These associations enable development teams to improve information sharing, capture institutional knowledge, and simplify regulatory compliance - which, in turn, translate into building significant business value.

Issue tracking in an agile environment will vary greatly depending upon an organization's software development environment. For some agile teams an agile project management tool will be sufficient.

But for teams working in large, complex, distributed or regulated environments, integrating the agile project management tool with either a bug tracking or ALM platform provides the best solution.

Issue Tracking in an Agile Development Environment

The term "issue tracking software" is most often associated with a bugtracker. However, in software development, the definition of an "issue" is much broader. An issue can be a bug; however, it can also be an enhancement, impediment, user story, development task, and more. In its broadest sense, an issue is anything that functionally needs to be addressed or delivered within a product release cycle.

As more organizations embrace agile methods for software development, they are turning to agile project management tools to help them manage the many issues that will arise during the course of a software release cycle. So how exactly do Agile project management tools handle issue tracking, and what are some of the advantages they bring?

It might be helpful to first look at how agile teams work. Let's assume that an organization is using Scrum, the most popular Agile method, for their agile software development. Scrum teams work in "sprints" - which are typically two to four week periods.

The feature requests that are to be completed in each sprint are written up as "stories" and placed in the product backlog, which is groomed and prioritized by the product owner. At the end of each sprint, the team has produced an increment of potentially shippable product - in this case an increment of properly tested "software".

As "issues" arise - and they will - during sprints, agile teams attempt to deal with them and course correct immediately, rather than wait until the end of the entire product build.

These issues might be impediments discovered during the daily scrum, bugs, or change requests and, similar to features, the issues are entered as stories into the product backlog.

Agile teams feel the best approach for dealing with bugs and other high priority issues is not to separate them from "features", but, rather, to include them in sprints along with features.

In this way, before a feature can be signed off, the issues associated with that feature must be resolved and closed. So in a sense, for agile development teams the distinction between bugs and features becomes less important, and the product backlog becomes in a sense - just a list of things people want.

Agile project management tools are designed to help agile teams manage the complexity of dealing with these large backlogs of features and issues in a software release.

After issues and enhancements are written up as stories, drag and drop interfaces in the agile tools make it easy for product owners to work with the team to prioritize stories, move their priority up in the backlog or drag them into the next sprint.

Burndown charts another simple, but powerful feature of an agile tool, help provide visibility into the progress a team is making on tackling issues and features across one sprint, several sprints or the entire release. Burndown charts allow teams to see the projected release dates and time remaining.

If teams find that they are dealing with particularly complex issues that may delay release, they may choose to adjust the scope of the project accordingly. By using agile tools that allow teams to manage issues alongside features, agile teams strive to minimize project risk, and increase the odds of producing a more reliable, higher quality product.

Chapter 12

Agile Estimation

Every project has its own uncertainty and no matter which methodology you choose there will be some degree of unpredictability, especially early on in a project. Agile methodology which relies heavily on team coordination, communication can help you set expectations and manage that uncertainty. Over the years organizations have implemented agile methods to varying degrees, to increase speed to market their product, increase productivity, growth strategy, improve operation effectiveness processes, improve product quality etc.

Many organizations that are new to agile process seem to struggle with estimation. It's important to clear the air about Agile estimation and how it can provide results if implemented in a right way.

1. Customer reads story.

2. Team estimates.
   This includes testing effort.

3. Team discusses.

4. Team estimates again.
   Repeat until consensus reached.

Estimates can help an organization to set a goal and expectations about what a team can deliver, but due to lack of poor planning teams struggle with estimation. In many cases, it has been observed that things turn out to be really rough if things are estimated without proper planning and understanding that may eventually jeopardize the whole project.

It's a proven fact that to make a precise prediction in a project you need to have a correct estimation. There are lot of things that need to be taken into consideration while calculating budget in any project like infrastructure, time frame, man hours etc. to get an idea of a plan and a goal to measure against. Once in a project you set a goal, teams need to come up with plans and estimate tasks.

A method that has been widely used in agile methodology to correct flaws in estimation techniques is planning poker. Planning poker theory sometimes called Scrum poker is a simple but powerful process that corrects any false precision and makes team-estimating faster, more accurate, and more fun. However it has a 'con' side to it.

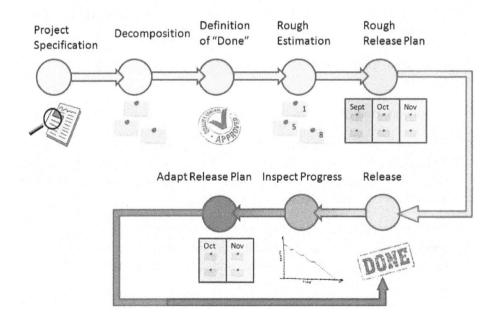

The estimating stories with Scrum poker theory is based on the story's complexity. A story for example with number 5 can be more cumbersome to complete than one that's has a number 3, but it doesn't meant that the 5 will take more time than 3 to complete. Estimates that are totally based on time can sometimes make planning commitments complex and uncertain.

Following are the key issues of the agile estimation process that most teams underestimate:

• Overlooking review effort, inspection and testing process

• Not to take into consideration the importance of having paper documentation

• Underestimating cost that include expenses like travel and meeting costs (especially large projects)

• Missing special testing requirements

• Underestimating project management / support effort, retrospective and demo meeting

• No plan for resistance after delivery if in case a support period is required

• Poor communication and team structure

It is pivotal that a team before the start of a project should do some basic research such as to collect important information about the requirements, do some thinking about the outcome, and then put this information through an estimation algorithm of choice.

Estimation is a complex process and if the planning and understanding is good in a team so will be the estimation. An estimate in the context of an agile project is all about shared understanding of requirement and solution.

Chapter 13

Distributed Teams Challenges And Agile Advantages

With dynamically changing market scenarios dominating the outsourcing markets, it has become imperative to remain conversant with emergent technologies and use them for developing projects.

New platforms and technologies have a lot to offer in terms of reduced development time and targeting a wider range of client-centric requirements, however, while reaping the benefits they offer, they also impose a few constraints regarding their applicability.

Offshoring businesses can increase the productivity levels and generate higher profits but often face problems in finding technical teams familiar with the usage and implementation of new technologies.

For most organizations, it is more profitable to find technical talent in other countries and outsource their projects depending upon the nature and scope of the project on hand.

It is very important to manage projects in an effective manner to make them profitable. Several project management frameworks and methods aim to make project management easier and more effective. Some of the popular methods used in the past, and even now are:

• Critical Path Method (CPM)

• Critical Chain Project Management (CCPM)

• PMI/PMBOK Method

• Event Chain Methodology (ECM)

• Extreme Project Management (XPM)

• Adaptive Project Framework (APF)

• Lean Development (LD)

• Six Sigma/Lean Six Sigma

• PRINCE2

• Dynamic Systems Development Model (DSDM)

• Feature Driven Development (FDD)

• Rapid Application Development (RAD)

• Systems Development Life Cycle (SDLC)

• Waterfall (Traditional)

Each method proposes to make project management easy and more accurate. Often, it is difficult to choose which method one ought to adopt for developing a project since every management technique has its own pros and cons.

While a particular organization may offer a positive feedback regarding a method it is following, consultants might consider it a bad choice and speak against it. There are no postulates or rules which define a "successful" project.

Also, there are no rules which can help in deciding whether a particular methodology is more effective as compared to the other. It is based more upon personal experience, understanding how a methodology works and what it has to offer, and how well it can be implemented.

Perhaps, the most important aspect to understand is whatever methodology you choose, what is more important is how well you use it to your benefit to make your project successful.

Projects may vary in terms of their scope, size, complexity, and nature. However, regardless of that, offshore or distributed teams have to be properly coordinated and managed. Agile project management framework offers several options for managing remotely developed projects.

Agile frameworks

Scrum

Recommended for developing small to medium sized projects using a team of 7 to 12 cross-functional and multi-skilled individuals. The Scrum framework is characterized by its clearly defined events, artefacts, roles, and process which have to be followed by the entire team.

The error correction and retrospection activities take precedence over documentation and delegation of authority. The client is actively involved in verifying the development carried out by the team. The Scrum team delivers the business value in the project through successful product increments developed through periodic cycles known as sprints.

Extreme Programming (XP)

Extreme Programming (XP) offers a practical approach to program development and focuses primarily upon the delivery of business results. It follows an incremental, start-with-something approach towards product development, and makes use of continued testing and revision processes.

XP is generally recommended for short-term projects, and development teams typically follow code-test-analyse-design-integrate process. XP is known for "paired" programming i.e. two developers engaged with code development and testing simultaneously. One programmer creates the code while other tests it on the spot.

Kanban

Based upon the concept of Toyota production model, Kanban offers a pragmatic approach to development by matching the actual amount of work in progress to the development teams capacity in delivering it.

The framework provides more flexibility in terms of planning options, quicker output, a clear focus pertaining what needs to be developed, and maintaining total transparency throughout the product development cycle.

Scaled Agile Frameworks (SAFe)

Scaled Agile Framework (SAFe) is a structured and prescriptive method to help large organisations and enterprises to get started with adopting Agile. It is a popular and efficient Agile framework successfully used by many companies covering various industry verticals. It is specially recommended for large sized software based projects where teams can function interdependently.

Nexus

Nexus is an Agile framework focusing upon cross-team dependencies and team integration issues. It facilitates Agile implementation in complex and large scale projects. It functions as an exoskeleton and helps multiple

Scrum teams to integrate and pursue a common goal of delivering valuable product increments through sprints.

Each team delivers a certain business value to the client through each product increment cycle, and the teams achieve this by following Agile principles and process. Nexus is recommended for development teams consisting of over 100 individuals.

While executing your very first remote project, the most logical thing to do is to document the project vision and figure out how the team will deliver the project goals. Proper and effective communication is of paramount importance while explaining the goals and objectives to team members.

It is a simple and straightforward process most of the times, but while working with distributed teams, the cultural differences and varying language proficiency levels may often create constraints and lead to miscommunication as well as confusion.

This can be a common scenario in case of teams located in countries across different time zones and possess limited ability to communicate using a particular language. Individuals may find it difficult to understand and capture the exact project requirements and deliver code or functionality that does not fulfill end user requirements. Projects often fail because of these and other such technical and non-technical reasons.

Using Agile it may be possible to simplify these types of problems. Agile is not a silver bullet that can rectify all issues and problems faced during project execution.

Agile is a framework, therefore It depends upon how well the team understands its principles and how effectively it implements them in the project. However, the framework is designed such that issues can be dealt with in a more proactive and effectual manner.

Chapter 14

Framework For Dealing With Issues Using Agile

Businesses opt for remote or distributed teams mainly to segregate the development activity from the main organization body by trans-locating the team and development activity to some other location for management or financial reasons.

The team is directly employed by the organization and each member is an employee. In case of offshoring, the entire project is outsourced to a development vendor who executes the project on behalf of the client, or develops it as a part of client contract. This discussion does not try to differentiate between whether the remote team is a part of parent organization or it belongs to an outsourcing vendor.

Some common issues faced while working with both types of teams are discussed and how those issues can be properly targeted using Agile. It is worthwhile to know that Agile is not the only project management platform to develop IT or software projects.

Neither does it offer a guaranteed way of dealing with issues faced while working with or employing remote teams. However, the framework is uniquely designed, and is flexible enough, to deal with such issues in a more effective manner, and more easily.

Project vision and documentation

The project vision explains the goals and project deliverables. The primary aim of the team should be to deliver work supporting the vision so meaningful business value can be delivered to the client.

Often, development teams put in efforts and deliver work, but when reviewed by the client, it is discovered that the features developed don't exactly support what the client actually wants.

This can be a very common scenario when teams are unclear about what the project aims to achieve and why it exists in the first place. Common reason why teams may fail to understand the vision could be language barriers (In case of distributed teams located in different countries and speaking different languages) or a lack of proper communication from the client's or management's side explaining the objectives.

Agile does not emphasize upon extensive documentation. In real life scenarios elaborate or extensive documentation often remains locked away in filing cabinets or resides on shelves for future references - teams rarely bother to read them thoroughly since they can be large in size and a lot of time is spent in reading and understanding them.

The attitude of most development teams (Don't mean to disrespect them in any way) is to get started with work so deadlines can be met. Teams are generally pressed for time so they don't bother, or can't afford to spend hours reading comprehensive documentation.

Paperwork is greatly reduced in Agile, and if you choose to follow Agile, you need to create just enough documentation to get started with work. More importance is given to understanding client-centric requirements and delivering business value, rather than creating elaborate reports and documents.

Moreover, one of the responsibilities of the product owner in Agile is to ensure that the team understands the deliverables and project vision properly before it starts to work. The PO also makes sure that the business value delivered from the sprints is useful and matches the project vision.

Maintaining quality standards

Quality and deadlines are two most important factors associated with, and affecting, the success levels of a project. Quality features fulfilling end user requirements have to be developed within the decided time so it can be properly marketed and business returns availed from it.

In the IT market segment it is not just important to build quality software, but to release it in the correct manner at the correct time and at the correct place (targeted market audience i.e. the geographical boundaries within which end users are likely to buy your product.

With online marketing these boundaries remain virtual but nevertheless play an important part in deciding the "target audience" when the project is planned and incepted). When outsourcing work to remote teams, the quality aspects could get compromised upon if a QA or testing process in set up as a part of development process.

Fewer development teams actually bother to test the code for regression after it is developed unless it is a pre-decided activity and integrated with the development process.

The Agile manifesto states "Our highest priority is to satisfy the customer through early and continuous delivery of valuable software." It emphasis upon "early and continuous delivery of valuable software" i.e. useful and valuable product features should be developed and delivered to the client on regular basis. Agile focuses upon the delivery of "shippable" features.

Each feature should be properly tested for errors and made bug free before its development can be considered as complete and deployable. Developers and programmers often double as testers to carry out the QA part during sprint cycles.

Agile fails if "workable" features are not developed. Remote teams trained in Agile have to fulfill the test conditions stated in the acceptance criteria defined for each development task created in the product backlog (ideally).

The supervisor or project manager's role

Every project needs a manager to oversee its execution and completion. It is important for the supervisor or the project manager to remain available to the team and resolve problems and issues as and when they occur.

When teams are located on-premises it becomes easy to resolve technical problems since face-to-face interactions are possible and the manager is always available when you need him or her. That is not always the case with remote or distributed teams.

Owing to time differences, the manager could be ending the day while the remote team would be just about to start with work. Teams may be required to wait for some time before problems are resolved, and this could delay work further. Deadlines and commitments may therefore not be met.

The Scrum Master's role is very clearly defined in Agile framework. The SM often plays a servant-leader role, and mentors and facilitates the Agile process. The SM ensures that he or she is always available to the team and resolves glitches whenever the team gets stuck.

In Agile, the Scrum Master is a specific role played by a person, rather than a designation or responsibilities given to a single individual. The role can be played by anyone in the team.

In case of distributed teams, a responsible team member can be taught to play the Proxy Scrum Master's role and provided with quick-access channels to communicate with the actual SM or PO in case of urgent issues. The person also functions as a team representative and creates daily feedback reports which can be studied by the client, PO, and the SM as per their convenience.

Ownership and team empowerment

Traditional project management methods differentiate between senior and junior level individuals, and have a clear hierarchical structure defining authority levels and who reports to whom.

Even today, most organizations still follow this traditional hierarchical model, and individuals belonging to different levels of authority remain concerned about their responsibilities and reporting status.

Even though the model is organized, it takes a lot of time for issues to get resolved as the escalation process involves several individuals starting from the junior level to senior levels. Moreover, people have a tendency to "pass on" issues to senior levels personnel and let them decide what to do next.

Technical staff and junior level employees may prefer not to get involved with decision making since they often become scapegoats to bureaucratic procedures.

In case of distributed teams the scenario can become even worse because you don't have to deal with just bureaucratic attitudes but the language and distance factor may further make the team even less accountable for the success or failure of the project.

Agile does not believe in shifting responsibilities or escalating issues. As per the model, teams are cross-functional and self-managing. Each team member often takes up additional tasks other than his or her particular skillset thereby reducing the total numbers of skilled members required in the team.

There are no senior-subordinate levels - just three primary roles of product owner, scrum master, and the development team. Rather than assigning tasks, each team member voluntarily takes up work based upon his or experience and skills.

One of the most important aspect about Agile is that the team has to "own" the project on behalf of the client. It means each person is responsible not just for the work done by him or her, but the overall contribution of all members at the team level is even more important. The entire team is accountable for the success or failure of the project - not just the product owner but each and every member of the team.

Moreover, the three roles of PO, SM, and the team are empowered in Agile to decide on their own what course of action to take to best fulfill their objectives.

The development team is not required to follow orders or take permissions in deciding how a particular feature should be developed, and in what manner. It has to deliver work as decided in an event - the sprint planning meeting - held before each product incremental cycle known as a sprint starts.

Chapter 15

Challenges Due To Agile Implementation And Integration With Traditional Systems

Managers in an organization face challenges when they try implementing the agile system off software development. Especially in an organization that has been following the waterfall approach. Although they may find small projects easier to handle with agile, they find it hard to scale up the agile technique for large projects.

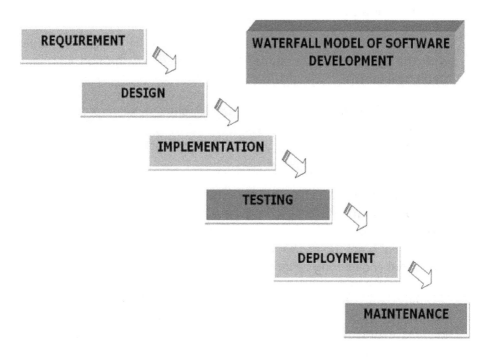

The major challenges that software project managers face in implementing agile can be categorized into three areas. These include areas concerning development related issues, business related issues, and people/ personnel related issues.

The challenge is further intensified if both traditional and agile approaches exist for different projects within the same organization.

Both approaches have different project and client attributes and modifying the organization's own attributes from project (agile) to project (traditional) is difficult. In this situation the issue areas include technology and processes too, apart from business and personnel.

Challenges in Agile Implementation in an Organization

Development Related Issues: The problem involves the challenge of 'merging together'. The agile is a lightweight process while the organizational processes are complicated and heavyweight as per the requirements of the traditional approach. How to suit agile to traditional complexity is a challenge in itself.

There is variability in subsystems and there may be integration issues with the elements of the same product developed through agile and traditional means.

There are differences in assumptions, GUI, choices, value proposition of both techniques leading to variability in features, and design at the time of delivery. Variation occurs in the life cycle of projects as the agile process has immediate release.

The traditional process has delivery scheduled after a long period. Issues also come from difference in requirement analysis of both techniques. The agile process has informal and functional requirement approaches which might not fit in the validation and verification method of the traditional engineering system.

Business Related Issues: The day to day operational process of both techniques vary. This might lead to issues associated with resource loading, estimation, and calculation variability. Agile personnel require enhanced skill and experience.

HR procedures in a traditional set up might not encourage people to pursue the non-traditional approach as this requires redefinition of organizational policy and processes. Since agile is iterative, traditional progress (design review) measurement ways are inadequate.

In agile requirement/feature completion can be used for progress measurement. Due to low documentation and infrastructure support, agile method does not comply with the standard requirements for CMMI, ISO or other process standards.

Personnel Related Issues: The major challenge can be a shift in attitude from traditional to agile. Traditional approach assigns employees to specific, well defined roles; while agile team members need to multitask. Agile project managers act as a coach and provide technical help when needed and the traditional PM generally delegates.

Logistic challenges relate to the need for a paired programming work station. Prompt handling of successful agile projects should be done to prevent destroying the technical and personal strengths of teams. The team of agile should consist of strong performers. A high degree of customer involvement, integration, and feedback involves dealing with challenge of synchronization among stakeholders.

Challenges for Organizations Following Traditional and Agile for Software Development

Organizations who seek to incorporate both the agile and traditional approach face issues pertaining to organizational framework adjustments, changes in technical and procedural requirements, management, and personnel related changes.

As discussed above, new competency development is required for adjusting to procedural and technical challenges. Learning requirements and the time period to make adjustments to skill enhancement for dealing with this challenge can be low. Adjustment requirements for culture, strategy, and framework, is large and a continuous process.

People issues relate to high levels of dynamism required in agile team. Issues may come up due to role inter-changeability, self-organization, and working on areas in which a developer might not be proficient.

The project manager's role changes from that of a strategist, controller, and allocator to that of a mentor and coach who collaborates and integrates the team. The highest degree of creativity requires a high level of ownership and leadership qualities.

This is in contrast to traditional teams existing within the same organization where competencies are formed around a process within a restricted set up and documentation. Existence of two opposing cultures of operation might lead to confusion and shake the organizational framework.

Organizational culture variation and difference in reward system of agile and traditional may lead to challenges. This may lead to development of various small-cultures within the organizational set-up. Adjustment of organizational framework to elements of dual culture might get difficult to handle.

Existence of a dual reward system where focus shifts from individual accomplishment to team accomplishment might get problematic. Such factors may pose serious hurdles to peaceful co-existence of following agile and traditional methodology of software development.

Optimization achievement and agility maintenance at the same time becomes difficult. Coexistence of both systems would mean both exploitation and exploration, both differing in behavior focus, hence are mutually exclusive.

It is essential to reconcile the differences between the two methodologies to truly develop an innovative, accommodating, and efficient system within stability and standard set up.

Chapter 16

Differences Between Agile And Waterfall Project Management

Agile software development is a concept or methodology that involves iterative development in short cycles. It includes a high level of interaction with users or business representative, and its flexible response to change is a positive for both business teams and project teams.

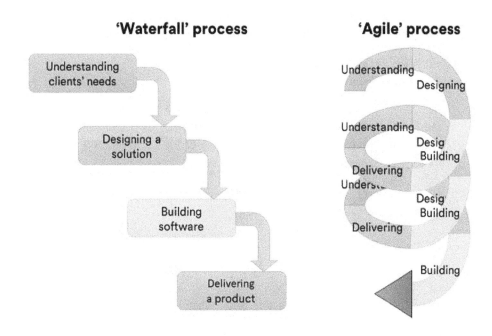

Agile development is based on a concept known as the Agile Manifesto, which is:

We are uncovering better ways of developing software by doing it and helping others do it. Through this work we have come to value:

Individuals and interactions over processes and tools

Working software over comprehensive documentation

Customer collaboration over contract negotiation

Responding to change over following a plan

That is, while there is value in the items on the right, we value the items on the left more.

As it says, the agile development process has different values than other software development methodologies. The other main software development methodology you may be familiar with is waterfall.

What Is Waterfall Software Development

Waterfall software development is a development process that involves stages that are run from start to finish before commencing the next stage. These stages are generally classified as:

1. Requirements - gathering the requirements of the system and what needs to be developed

2. Design - designing the system

3. Implementation - developing the software system

4. Verification - testing the system, both system testing and user testing

5. Maintenance - ongoing support or maintenance of the system

In this methodology, the requirements are gathered at the start of the project, with the aim of confirming them at the start to reduce cost and time impact later in the project. It is a common belief that finding discrepancies and issues earlier in the project will result in less time being spent than if they were found later in the project.

Waterfall is the more traditional method of development. It was the main methodology that was taught in schools and universities (at least when I was there!) and depending on your company, it's the one that is most commonly used.

However, there is discussions among the IT industry about agile vs waterfall - what are the differences, and which is better?

What is the difference between agile and waterfall?

Agile uses iterations, waterfall uses stages

Agile has constant business interaction, waterfall has varied high and low interaction (high during requirements and user testing, low during development and system testing)

Agile has roles such as scrum master, waterfall has project manager

Can't go back with Waterfall, can with agile

There are several key differences between the agile methodology and waterfall methodology, which are:

Agile uses iterations, waterfall uses stages. The agile process uses short iterations, known as "sprints", which generally last between 4 and 6 weeks. The requirements are confirmed, system is developed and tested, and released during this iteration, and the next one begins. With the waterfall process, the requirements are all set at the start, and then the next stage begins

Once a stage is finished with waterfall, you can't go back. If you've finished the requirements phase and obtained signoff from the business users, the requirements phase is over. There is no going back - unless a change process is followed which can take time. With agile, if requirements need to change, they are better handled with this process.

Agile requires constant business interaction for the entire cycle, waterfall has high and low points. For each agile sprint or cycle, constant interaction with users and business stakeholders is needed - which can be difficult to get if you're not in the same area or if there is no support from their manager.

With the waterfall methodology, the business interaction is needed up front (with the requirements gathering) and then again at the user testing stage - and not a lot in between. This can be a good and a bad thing.

Agile roles are different to waterfall roles. Roles in an agile project are generally different to those in a waterfall project. Agile has a role called a Scrum Master, which is a kind of project manager and release manager, and may not be an IT person. Waterfall has a traditional project manager, which is almost always an IT person in the traditional sense.

Which Is Better - Agile Vs Waterfall

This chapter brings us to our last point - comparing agile vs waterfall. This depends on several factors, such as the work environment and the style of project.

Agile methods are more suited to those projects that need small and frequent functionality delivered to the users. It is also suited to those projects where delivery time to market needs to be considered.

Waterfall methods are suited to those projects where a high level of business involvement is not possible or not needed, and where quality is more important than speed to market. This isn't to say agile results in poorer quality projects - it just means that as there is a dedicated testing phase, it places more emphasis on it.

The experience of the project team also needs to be considered - whether they have experience delivering or working on agile projects, as this will be a big help. One of the tips on how to become a good software developer is to be knowledgeable in both agile and waterfall methodologies.

Whether you're into product design, software engineering, construction or any other industry, there is usually more than one way to get things done. In terms of project management, the two most prolific methods for getting things done are the classic waterfall style of project management and the new kid on the block, agile project management.

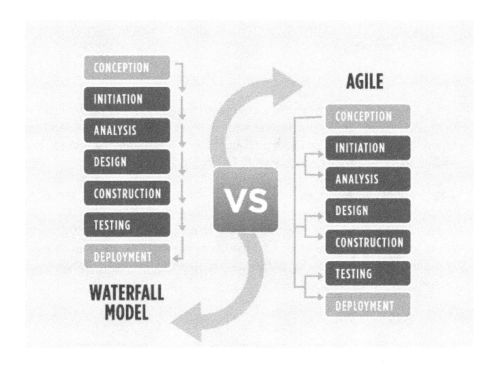

To decide which is best for your needs, you need to develop a solid understanding of the advantages and limitations of each type of project management technique. Here we investigate what is different about the two schools of thought, and compare side by side the advantages and limitations of each.

Waterfall project management mimics the normal workflow process in any manufacturing or construction project as it is a sequential process. Each of the stages happens in isolation, and once complete, the team move on to the next stage in the sequence.

• Advantages

Waterfall project management relies upon meticulous record keeping. This means there is a clear paper trail to follow, allowing the process to be refined and improved upon in the future.

From the outset, the client will have a clear idea of what is going to happen during project delivery. They will know roughly what the cost, timescales and size of the project will be, and will have a good idea of what to expect in the end.

• Limitations

Once a stage in the process has been completed, there is no way to go back and change things without scrapping the whole project and starting again. The whole process relies on robust initial requirements; if these are flawed then the project is doomed to failure from the outset.

The product is developed in stages and only tested fully at the end, meaning bugs may be so ingrained in the end product that they are impossible to remove. Finally, this type of project management doesn't allow for changes to the brief, so if the client realises they need to change the brief half way through, sacrifices will need to be made in terms of budget and timescales.

Agile methodology

Agile was once touted as the solution to many of the problems in waterfall project management. Rather than following a sequence of steps in isolation, this method relies upon an incremental approach to the project delivery.

Project teams start off with a very simple concept of where they are going, and then work on discreet modules in short 'sprints'. At the end of each sprint the modules are tested to discover any bugs or flaws and customer feedback is gathered before the next sprint takes place.

• Advantages

Plenty of changes can be made after initial plans are developed, in fact rewrites and major changes are almost expected. This makes it easier to add features and keep abreast of changes in the industry, even whilst the project is being delivered. Regular testing ensures flaws are identified early on, meaning that the product can be ready for launch more quickly and is more likely to be a quality product.

• Limitations

This method requires a strong project manager to keep things on track and balance out creativity with project delivery requirements. Because of the haziness of the original project plan, the final product can often end up being wildly different to what was originally intended.

Choosing a methodology

The two methods of project management both have their time and place, and the one which is best for your needs will depend entirely on your specific brief. When you know what a final product should be and are confident your client won't need to change the scope half way through, waterfall project management is your friend.

However if speed of production is more important than the quality of the finished product and the client wishes to be able to change scope part way through, agile allows for more flexibility and is one of the things every project manager should know about.

Chapter 17

Steps Integral To Making A Project Agile

The word agile denotes an ability to move quickly with a high level of flexibility and this very concept is embodied in agile methodologies adopted for software development and project management among other things.

Agile methodologies were originally developed in an effort to enhance the process of software development through an approach aimed at minimizing the time, resources and incidence of error in the final product.

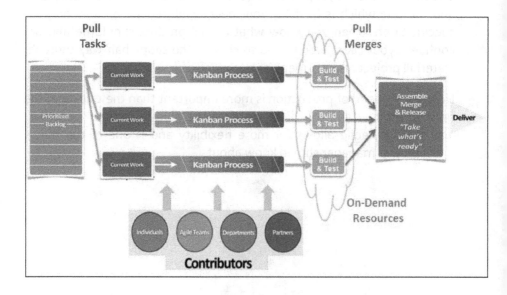

Traditionally, even slight changes in project requirements could upset the whole development cycle and it would be difficult to predict the quality of outcome and the time spent on fixing any possible errors.

However, agile processes helped reducing the development life cycle into manageable delivery cycles in which the software product could be developed in functional segments and tested for any possible flaws to ensure that they are working as required.

How Agile Methodologies Can Be Of Help?

This approach allowed the Developers to assimilate almost any big or small changes at any stage of the project without affecting the quality of the end product. In this way product functionalities could be tested, reviewed and improved upon much in advance of delivering the end product in its entirety.

This led to major cost reductions and lesser time was spent on taking corrective measures in the final stages of project with overall improved efficiency resulting in a win-win situation.

Project Managers were quick to realize that agile methodologies could have industry-wide applications and by adopting agile processes non-IT project management could also be made that much more efficient and cost-effective.

Some of the steps integral to making a project agile are:

Scan:

At the first sign of change, agile development relies on keeping an eye out for emerging trends and patterns which can help understand new conditions better.

Analyze:

Take into account any new information and knowledge available and chalk out plans accordingly. This would help keep pace with changing conditions and not be left behind in work goals.

Respond:

After identifying areas that present potential risks and opportunities, develop responsive strategies to take advantage of opportunities and mitigate risks.

Change:

Transforming existing policies and processes with a view to make them more inclusive in terms of ongoing changes and enhance overall adaptability of the workflow as a result.

Traditional Sequential Project Management, also known as Waterfall Project Management is best suited for projects where level of uncertainty is comparatively low and requirements are not supposed to change much in the duration of project.

On the other hand, Agile Project Management thrives on assimilating change and exploring diverse solutions to make the project development more flexible and overcome unforeseen hurdles at any stage of development process.

Efficient collaboration and communication hold the key to setting agile development in motion by bringing everyone on board and helping understand the approach embodied in agile processes. The project development is broken up in various segments and tasks are sub-divided and smaller time segments are assigned for completing each of these tasks.

This is known as incremental project development, allowing for review at every stage of development instead of waiting for project completion. After every stage of the project, the design and functionality of completed project tasks can be evaluated against current requirements and suitable improvements can be made.

The tasks can then be re-evaluated at regular intervals and in this way, improvement, innovation and diversification in terms of solutions become the basis for development in an ongoing project.

This leads to efficient utilization of available time and resources and creates greater space for experimentation and exploring alternatives wherever traditional approaches to planning do not yield satisfactory results. These are also the reasons why agile development is so much in demand these days.

Whether it is software development, a construction project or a project leading to creation of any specific product or service, agile processes help enhance the productivity while working within the time and scope of the project. Through adoption of agile methodologies, an organization can not only make its processes more efficient but also improve its organizational culture as a whole.

Chapter 18

Benefits of Agile Software Development

Agile development is a strategy of software development in which the process occurs though short increments. The phases of the development process occur continuously in iterative cycles, involving a requirements phase, design and implementation, testing, and reporting.

Stakeholders and designers meet after each increment to discuss what has occurred, re-evaluate requirements and determine priorities. This allows for greater transparency between clients and programmers and clients have greater influence in what is being designed to ensure the product is what they want.

The traditional waterfall method general involves the stakeholders at the beginning requirements phase, and then the development company takes over and designs the website. The stakeholders or clients only see the finished product, which may or may not be what they had in mind.

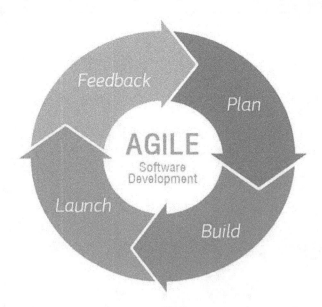

The many advantages to agile software development can improve the quality of work for a software development company.

While there can be some disadvantages if the client does not want to be involved in the entire process or the team is not good at communication, these issues can be worked out as the team gains experience with the process. Agile software development companies are on the rise as more research shows it is a productive method of producing usable and effective software.

Agile software development describes a unique approach to computer programming. The popularity of the concept really took off more than a decade ago in 2001 when a group of experienced software developers got together to document the best way to develop software.

This effort culminated in the Manifesto for Agile Software Development, a publication detailing the 12 core principles of this unique approach to creating software.

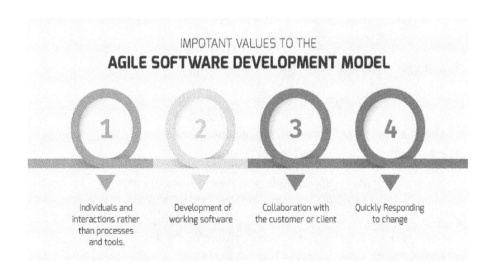

IMPOTANT VALUES TO THE
AGILE SOFTWARE DEVELOPMENT MODEL

1	2	3	4
Individuals and interactions rather than processes and tools.	Development of working software	Collaboration with the customer or client	Quickly Responding to change

Over the years, the popularity of the agile approach is increasing as individuals, project teams, and entire companies recognize a variety of benefits.

A primary feature of agile software programming involves breaking projects into a series of regular, predictable iterations, or development time periods (also referred to as "sprints"). While the length of these iterations may vary project to project and team to team, they typically last between 7 days and one month.

Agile software development is often contrasted with the waterfall approach to programming. One of the major differences between the two approaches involves the issue of software testing. In the waterfall approach, software is created and then tested just before implementation. With agile, software testing is done on an ongoing basis, repeatedly throughout the coding process.

The scrum framework is another popular methodology used by many teams engaged in the agile approach towards custom software development. This is an organized, collaborative approach that encourages cross-functional teamwork, regular communication, and a clear focus towards well-specified common goals.

Benefits of Agile Software Development and Scrum

The popularity of agile software programming has grown exponentially over the past decade for a number of different reasons, and there are now many champions of this approach. Follow along to learn five benefits of the agile approach to software development:

More Productivity - During agile software development, the workload is broken up into smaller chunks and the deliverables are completed in shorter iterations. This decreases the chance that programmers get too far off track on a project, and when problems do happen, they are more easily identified and corrected more quickly.

Increased Morale of Programmers - Many computer programmers prefer to do their work in smaller achievable pieces, rather than big overwhelming tasks that may lack clarification. This helps people recognize accomplishments and better measure progress which tends to increase overall morale both individually and on a team.

Clearer Communication - Both agile and scrum encourage clearer and more frequent communication between all of the business partners involved in a software project. The scrum framework establishes an organized process for daily communication and responsibility, creating tighter team bonds and greater project clarity.

Higher Quality - Agile and scrum often lead to a better end product because the project work is divided into smaller units which are easier to test and validate along the way. In the end, this typically leads to fewer errors and higher overall quality.

Predictable Costs - Because cost estimates are typically required at the beginning of each iteration in the agile software development work cycle, estimating costs tends to be easier and more transparent. Predictable costs also improve decision making about priority features and project changes.

While agile programming is dynamic and includes a range of approaches and preferences, the fundamental structure to agile software development yields some clear benefits for business leaders, software developers, project managers and others.

An increasing number of companies are seeking talented people trained in the agile and scrum approach and more software consulting and IT staffing firms are featuring career opportunities for individuals with these skillsets.

Given the many benefits of this unique approach to programming and project management, it is likely that the popularity of agile for developing software will only continue to increase.

Chapter 19

The Agile Software Outsourcing system

In the present times when we are living in an extremely competitive world, the field of Information Technology has more likely become the backbone of a large number of entities all around the globe which is truly useful in bringing up various other demands for effectiveness and efficiency in the total working process.

Making a general link to all, outsourcing is normally considered being one of the most helpful procedure in which a company is a part for its work to another entity.

Making it simple, it appears to be the creation of an equal liability and responsibility for the implementation as well as the design of the business processes by maintaining standardized directives that have been issued by the essential provider entity.

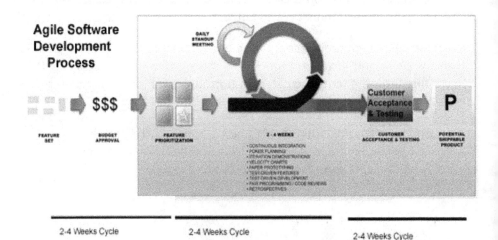

The Agile software outsourcing system happens to be extremely beneficial for both of the companies such as the service provider as well as the outsourcing company as it is helpful in minimizing the costs. It is also useful in increasing the quality of the various non-core business activities and also helpful for infusing the competence and expertise to the largest.

Most of all, the agile software outsourcing has truly become an extremely imperative economic activity for both the creation of the difference as well as for the countries all around the world.

Customized software development is actually the need of the present times. Information Technology as well as IT based businesses are getting through a great revolution and for this reason; new tools and different concepts concerning technology have been evolving to a great extent.

Every single IT based business entity is looking forward to make use of these customized tools in the technological manners so that they can easily offer their customer base with better and superior services. In case they do not have their own team to work on it then they certainly hold back an option to outsource or hire others for these purposes.

Agile software development basically is a particular framework that is being used for a large number of software development projects. It actually came out of frustration within the conventional project management activities. It has been now considered as a vital tool for the growth and development of the business enterprises.

The agile software development firms are trying their best to provide people with an access to professional and specialized essence to the nerves of the waving and smoothing information technology to incarcerate.

The process of agile software development can even be outsourced. One of the primary advantages you are going to get by agile software outsourcing is that it happens to be an exceptionally cheap labor involvement, timeliness, efficiency in the work and various other benefits that would be possible to the earliest.

While a particular set of software development methodologies and techniques are being utilized, in such cases the solutions arise as a result of collaborative and mutual team work which certainly happens to be cross-functional and such kinds of methodologies are called as the agile software development.

Such teams and groups mostly focus more on the various faces of communications instead of the written communication faces that are useful to make sure that the project is going to its right and accurate direction.

In case of an agile software outsourcing, it is a lot better to make arrangements for video-conferencing or tale-interviews periodically so that project checks and updates could be easily acquired and any modifications can be implemented right on time without any sort of delays.

Right away from the project's planning phase, requirements analyses, designing, unit testing, encodings, and final prototypes that are useful in figuring out any kinds of errors will be run before it is going to be showcased in front of the valuable consumers.

Such sort of a mutual team work throughout the project development phase truly is crucial for any business entity and it is helpful in reducing the overall risks. In case there are some modifications that are to be integrated, they can be easily managed and will be carried out right on time without any delays.

Equal importance is given to comprehensive and detailed documentation of the project by these agile software outsourcing companies. This makes it extremely helpful in case at some later date when they want to make some necessary changes, they could easily incorporate them.

Agile software outsourcing is an approach through which various organizations use the power of the internet combined with a tested methodology to get inexpensive labor. Agile represents a real-time software creation technique used to conquer the shortcomings of the conventional software development process.

Agile software outsourcing is a tool that many outsourcing companies use currently to stop producing monotonous outcomes. They want to explore the global talent while making sure that they give their clients real agile approaches.

The agile methodology is versatile enough to allow a few remote teams to work together on a single project. This guarantees that a project owner would get an output that does not only boasts uniqueness but also a high level of creativity.

While the internet allows an organization to employ professionals from any country, caution must be exercised when selecting the most appropriate service providers. The most qualified service providers must promise to clients the following six things:

A short time of software development - The hired provider must establish that its infrastructure has all the resources needed to produce quick and error-free results.

An early Return on Investment (ROI) - The outsourced company must demonstrate how it can mobilize its team to work quickly and effectively to produce a market-ready product.

Help the client adapt easily to change - Today's local and global markets are volatile and require flexible software development techniques that can accommodate change.

The hired offshore software developer must provide total protection from the technical changes caused by the frequently growing Information Technology (IT). It must prove that its resources and infrastructures are constantly updated with the latest technologies.

Increase business growth - The main reason why agile software outsourcing is done is to encourage business growth.

Companies sub-contract work to low-priced professionals to eliminate the costs of hiring more staff, avoid using outdated problem-solving models and to attempt to attain better performance levels. The service provider must demonstrate how its final software can boost the growth of the client's business.

Increase the customer's involvement in every development stage - The customer must know about each agile iteration (refers to one development cycle measured as one or two weeks) to remove mistakes or add suggestions in advance.

This can help the team members to work accurately and confidently toward the final goal. This is unlike the traditional software development process that involves the clients only in the first stages and so the errors are noticed after the completion of the project.

Minimize the development risks - Software creation costs are among the highest expenditures incurred by companies. Even if delegating the development duties to global teams is a cheaper alternative, a company must investigate further various service providers. It is important to engage a programmer who has many years of proven experience so as to reduce the risks of getting low quality software eventually.

To draw close remote teams that are doing one project, the recruiting company must get rid of communication barriers. Today there are many communication modes that can be used to make agile software outsourcing successful. These include consistent video conferencing, chatting, emailing and VoIP call interviewing among others.

Chapter 20

Agile Implementation Principles To Secure Project Success

Business stakeholders want something when they want it; they don't care how well the project adhered to a particular development methodology. Agile principle adherence shouldn't become the focus of the project. It is the vehicle in which a project gets implemented, not the reason for the project.

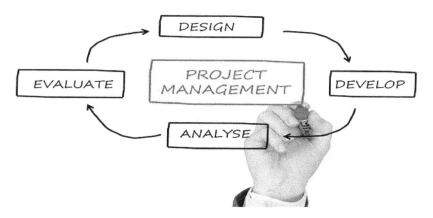

Agile doesn't mean skipping any kind of testing, particularly integration and regression testing. It just means you are compressing and overlapping and being less "over the wall" in test stages. Successful agile requires focused business user involvement through design, development, and testing. None of this "let me know when it's done" stuff.

Top down project management orchestration is crucial. Empowering teams is important, but can't be taken to a point of anarchy.

Depending on where an organization is at in its systems development methodology journey, it may not be able to jump to a purist agile model and be successful. I've learned that the following six principles are paramount in a successful agile project.

Embedded Power User - Having an experienced and forward-thinking dedicated user who can guide capability development and bring other users to the table as needed ensures that the capabilities under development will align to the business and will minimize capability gaps after implementation.

Time Fences - Rather than having team members set their own delivery dates, the project team needs to work to defined time fences and flex the work to hit the time fence. Key to this is the project manager having some flexibility to alter a time fence if it makes sense to do so.

Governing Architecture - I watched an agile project with six capability teams go off the rails because each team was given too much architectural freedom of choice.

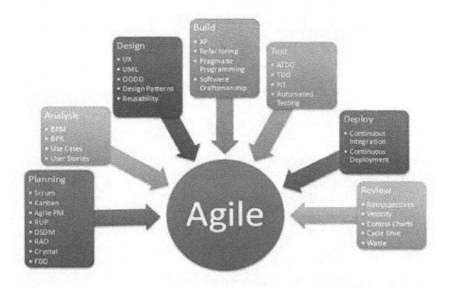

About five sprints into the project the capabilities didn't fit together because of individual decisions made by capability teams, creating massive rework. There needs to be a concise functional and technical architecture that capability teams must snap to.

Small, Frequent Deployments - I like executing plans that have monthly capability releases. It keeps the energy going, gives business users and stakeholders something to look forward to each month, and gives everyone something to celebrate each month.

Persistent Testing - Developers tend to like "grand reveals." where a capability isn't shown to others until the developer is sure everything works 100%. I prefer to have testing and power users involved as close as possible to development to find problems early on.

There is a big trust issue that has to be overcome when you take this approach; the developer needs to not be randomized by "Are you done yet?" questions and needs to know that if something breaks during development the power user won't start launching flares that the product is of poor quality. The developer, in turn, needs to avoid the grand reveals where fixing problems later in the schedule becomes more expensive.

Strong Project Management - Agile isn't code for anarchy, and it's not a time when the PM is relegated to administrative errand-running.

The PM needs to be driving accountability, ensuring issues are being addressed, risks are being mitigated, dates are being met, and scope is being adhered. At the end of the day, the PM gets the first bullet if the project fails and needs to ensure everyone is doing his or her job to meet scope, schedule, and budget goals.

I've never seen a project manager get points because he or she followed the rules of agile on a failed project. The first and foremost goal is agreed-upon scope delivered on time and within budget.

Keep the above principles in mind as you take on your next agile implementation to better ensure success and not get tied up in whether or not you're doing agile right.

Chapter 21

Scopes of Agile Planning

The concept of planning within the agile methodology has often been misunderstood. Due to the commonly known statement "We value responding to change over following a plan" most of teams starting agile think that they will no longer need to plan for the future. Contrary to this popular opinion, planning plays just as big of a part in agile as it does in any other project management approach it is simply a little different.

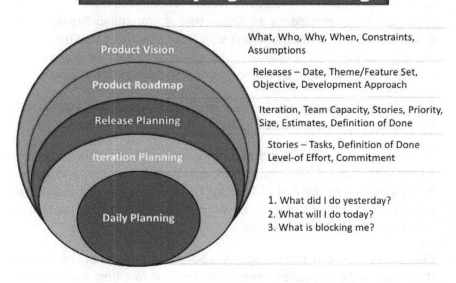

In its essence agile is built to cater the environments with constantly changing requirements and goals. Which means that the traditional planning model, of just setting something in motion at the beginning of the project, is no longer viable.

Instead, the planning needs to cater to the changing circumstances and help the team navigate them in the best possible way. To achieve this, the agile planning is organized in different scopes, where each of them are equally important and carry value towards the end goal.

First comes the product vision. This is the largest scope of the project planning and is usually handled by the management. They have to define what the project is all about, what is it they are trying to achieve and for which purpose.

While this may seem perfectly clear for the top management, without communicating such information to the people involved in a simple and concise way, the project may run off the desired course very quickly. Therefore to have a clear product vision is essential to any agile team.

Second - a product road map. The next largest scope of agile planning, helps to clarify which steps need to be taken to achieve the defined product vision. Simply put, the product roadmap is made up out of all the features that are required out of the finished project.

Based on their importance and priority they are put in a specific order and represent how the product will be built. This planning scope is particularly important for products that span over a longer period of time and have multiple releases.

Similar to the product road map, the next scope of planning is all about the release plan which defines how many releases the product will have. The release plan is not focused on features or dates, but ties directly with the scope of work to be completed. This planning step is important as it gives the teams more incentive to finish a specific product version, ensures the management of the progress and allows for larger fund and effort allocation.

After defining the vision, roadmap and the release plan for the project, the agile planning turns back to the teams completing the work. The next planning scope is on them, with a commonly known sprint planning.

Contrary to the previous planning scopes, this is done more frequently and directly relates to the day to day tasks of each employee. With that, it is also a more flexible planning event that (within the allocated borders) allows the team to react to any changes in requirements and circumstances and move forward to the project completion.

The fifth and the absolute smallest scope of agile planning is the daily standup. While some may see it just as an update, this is a planning event as well, defining the goals for the next day. This small planning event helps to ensure that the sprint plan is being executed well and that the team is not forgetting the overall vision of the product.

The planning of agile projects is different from the traditional waterfall planning we are used to having. Just like the methodology it is designed for change and for frequent updates. The different scopes of this planning approach ensures the team has clear goals set for the overall project and can easily plan their day to day work.

Planning activities for large-scale development efforts should rely on five levels:

Product Vision

Product Roadmap

Release Plan

Sprint Plan

Daily Commitment

The certainty of undertaking activities addressed in each of the five levels increases, and therefore the amount of detail addressed (money invested), the number of people involved and the frequency can increase without running the risk of spending money on features that may not be built or may be built differently. Each of the five levels of planning addresses the fundamental planning principles: priorities, estimates and commitments.

The broadest picture that one can paint of the future is a vision of a product owner. In this vision she explains how an organization or product should look. She indicates what parts of the system need to change (priority) and what efforts can be used to achieve this goal (estimates and commitments).

Product Visioning - How To

Possible structures for a visioning exercise are to create an elevator statement or a product vision box The principle of both exercises is to create a statement that describes the future in terms of desired product features, target customers and key differentiators from previous or competitive products.

For (target customer) who (statement of the need) the (product name) is a (product category) that (product key benefit, compelling reason to buy). Unlike (primary competitive alternative), our product (final statement of primary differentiation)."

The product vision describes a desired state that is 12 months or more in the future. Further planning (design) activities will detail the vision, and may divert from the vision because the future will bring us a changed perspective on the market, the product and the required efforts to make the vision reality.

Product Roadmap - Level 2

The era of large-scale projects that deliver results in years is behind us. Customers demand more frequent changes and typical time-to-market timeframes are measured in weeks or months.

The higher frequency and smaller timeframes force a product owner into thinking in steps, into thinking of a road towards the final product. Just like a journey is planned upfront and shared with the fellow travelers, a product roadmap is created and communicated to fellow delivery people.

The goals for doing so are for the product owner to:

Communicate the whole

Determine and communicate when releases are needed

Determine what functionality is sufficient for each release

Focus on business value derived from the releases

The delivery team on the other hand will:

See the whole

Learn about the steps to realize the vision

Learn the business priorities

Provide technical input to the roadmap

Provide estimates for the projected features

Product Roadmap - How To

The creation of the roadmap is largely driven by the product owner (or product owner team). This stage of the program has limited influence of technology constraints. In a meeting or series of meetings, the roadmap will be drawn by the product owner. This can be quite literally, through a graphical representation of the releases, or more formally in a written document outlining the dates, contents and objectives of the foreseen releases.

Product Backlogs

In anticipation of the next planning stage (release planning) a list of desired features needs to be built - the product backlog. In its simplest form, such a backlog is a table (spreadsheet) of product requirements, briefly described so a delivery team can provide estimates for the realization of each feature.

Most importantly, the list has to be prioritized. The success of an Agile development project depends on the early delivery of the highest priority features. Since the success of a project is measured in business terms, the prioritization of the feature list is the responsibility of the business, i.e. the product owner. Interaction with the delivery teams is required.

Without a discussion of the features it will be hard for the delivery team to produce estimates that have an acceptable inaccuracy. Characteristics of a product backlog include:

One product backlog for all teams (see the whole)

Large to very large features (up to 20 'person days' to deliver a feature)

Feature priority based on business priorities (discovered through market research)

Technology features (sometimes called non-functional features, work required to make the product work in a desired way, e.g. the implementation of a certain DBMS in order to warrant a certain system performance) are limited to those that have a direct impact on the success of the product in the market.

Chapter 22

What Every Manager Ought To Know About Agile Development

To the project team itself agile methods might look great, but convincing management and people that talk business sense it is a good thing is often a much harder process. I find this interesting because one of the main focuses of agile is to place the quality of software over everything else.

As a primary metric, agile and agile meta models (SCRUM for example), focus on making maximum business sense or providing maximum business value at the end of every iteration.

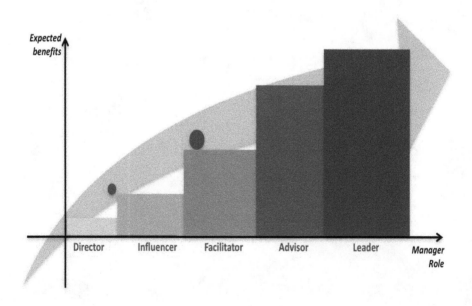

Ok, so agile makes it a standing point to deliver on what the customer wants at the end of each iteration, but what are the other motivating factors behind pushing agile as a model for delivering real business value.

An improved feedback and control loop

Agile provides its clients with frequent opportunities to provide feedback at the end of an iteration. With this, they can further direct the project in an incremental fashion, driving the next iteration with their business sense, asking questions like "What is of most business value to me right now?"

This iterative feedback from both the client and project team lead to advantages that would otherwise not be available, jumping on new and upcoming technologies and developments to spearhead the next iteration.

These changes and developments have the effect of spearheading the project towards success and an overall better product. In some cases, it can provide improved return on investment by allowing the product to be deployed much earlier. Remember, an iteration focuses on delivering the most business value it can.

If there is enough of that value there, enough to make this business sense just that, it is worth deploying early to start recouping on costs before the product has even reached the end of its development life cycle. By the time the project has come to completion, you may well have recouped half of your initial investment.

Avoid catastrophes

It's common for a project to be tracking well and suddenly fall behind at a late stage in development. Why? Traditional software development life cycle models find it much harder to judge the correctness and completeness of up front analysis and design.

This lack of information sometimes leads to overly optimistic views which don't manifest until much later in the project when it is too late to do anything about it. Do you cut your losses and get out? Or take the risk? Well, another way to look at it would be to avoid this risk altogether.

And by avoid, we really mean circumvent. As an iterative model, agile performs short bursts of analysis, design and implementation often. This gives rise to much more tracking data before entering the next iteration to re-evaluate where the project is at and if it is still on track.

The only four variables we really have control over in software development are: time, scope, cost and quality. Having the advantage of a model closely tied to these variables often and right throughout the projects life cycle is a big risk mitigator.

A focus on quality

This is a major area of agile models and comes back to core concepts known as the agile manifesto. It is basically saying; focus on quality software that translates into real business value for the customer each step of the way.

Deliver this value at the end of each iteration, even if it means less formal practices and documentation is kept. Use customer collaboration as an improvement mechanism and embrace any change that might be coming.

Like extreme programming agile also adopts the practice of pair programming. No discussion on "What makes good business value?" or "What brings good return on investment?" would be complete without talking about it. It's often hard convincing management that using two people on one task is beneficial.

The productivity of having two people on one task is slightly lower than each working individually (I'm not going to make up any fancy statistics here:)). So this would raise the argument that pair programming actually costs more! What you cannot as easily measure however is the increase in quality pair programming brings.

Agile promotes information sharing

All information is shared amongst team members, often with the activities being shared to: analysis, design and implementation (pair programming during development for example). This information loop routinely filters through to the customer too. After all, that's why they are there, to provide input going into the next iteration.

Agile development however is not necessarily well suited to all types of projects. Sometimes no matter how hard you try you just cannot come up with a good enough business reason to justify the model. That's fine, agile does not suit every type of project small and large. Just recognize when you might be able to gain the flexibility and momentum it offers.

Chapter 23

Establishing An Agile Dedicated Team

A dedicated development team is a software production and managerial staff who works for your company remotely (nearshore or offshore). Such a team is established on the basis of (or with help of) a local IT or specialized outstaffing firm. Normally such firms provide:

• IT specialists with required skills;

• Infrastructure: hardware, software, networks, office space, etc.;

• Necessary tax, accounting, and legal services for the team members;

• Administrative and technical support and supervision.

Every team member is selected by the customer. Usually the size and skill profile of a dedicated team can be changed with time.

To date a wide experience is accumulated in utilizing dedicated development teams located in Asia, Eastern Europe (Ukraine, Russia, Romania, etc.), and other popular outsourcing destinations. According to analytical reports, this model can be considered as one of the most reliable forms of IT outsourcing both for large companies and small software firms and start-ups from the USA and Europe.

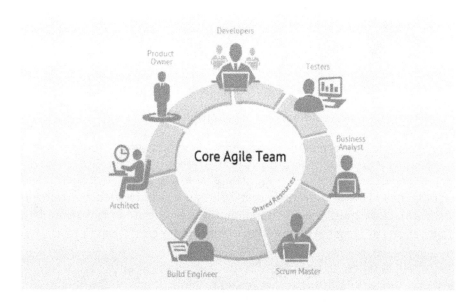

At the same time the practice demonstrates that in many cases the best results are achieved when the dedicated team model is united with Agile software development methodology.

Agile Development

Agile software development refers to a group of programming methodologies based on iterative development, where requirements and solutions evolve through collaboration between cross-functional teams. The term was coined in 2001 when the Agile Manifesto had been formulated.

The Manifesto accentuates close collaboration, ongoing communication, welcoming requirements change on any project stage, and customers' satisfaction as an ultimate goal of paramount importance.

Agile Dedicated Software Development Teams

Applying Agile approach to dedicated software development teams, we get outsourced software development which is characterized by the following points:

Common purposes and values for the customer and remote team

Iterative planning and development

Regular communication between the client and dedicated team

Early identifying and mitigating risks

Aspiration to finding solutions for every problem

Continuous learning, knowledge exchange and processes improvement

Agile dedicated teams are not just a sum of the above-mentioned approaches. This is a synergy that helps to mitigate such outsourcing risks as lack of mutual understanding, different treatment of tasks, late (and, as a result, costly) recognition that something isn't right, etc.

Establishing an Agile Dedicated Team

Here are some tips how to make an agile dedicated team more effective.

1. Build a proper team and team spirit

Choose experienced and educated stuff with good language skills to be double sure you are on the same line with them. The team members should accept criticism, tend to optimize the process and make it clearer for you at all stages. Another important thing to take into account is a team spirit and readiness to collaboration. Every member should respect the project goals.

2. Try to minimize the culture gap

Minimizing the culture gap is another way to save you time, money and nerves. Good language level and interpersonal skills of the team members help to ease communication and secure successful project completion. But if you are not strong in understanding different mentalities, try to work with countries which have cultural traditions close to yours.

3. Set up regular status meetings and open discussions

This will help you to understand where the project is at any given moment. In fact, open relations and close communication between you and the dedicated team are cornerstones of the software development project success.

4. Small iterations and continuous integration

Divide your project into small iterations and require regular software integration. This will give you more fine-grained control on the real project progress. You'll be able to scope portions of completed functionality and, as a result, find any misunderstandings, detect problems at the very early stage, and react in time by clarifying the requirements or fixing the code.

5. Check that the code is clean and documentation is well-structured

Well-shaped and commented source code is a key for further smooth maintenance. Also, that helps to keep the project responsive to requirement changes with minimal effort.

Proper documentation makes knowledge transfer easy and cost-effective. So, make sure the team members have relevant experience in source code design and documenting techniques.

Agile dedicated teams can essentially decrease risks typical for other outsourcing models. Really, here, the key activities in project management, software development and quality inspection are comprehensively controlled by the customer.

Being used properly the agile dedicated team model provides both the main benefits of nearshore/offshore IT outsourcing (such as cost savings) and a high level of control and confidence inherent for in-house software development processes.

Chapter 24

When Is Agile Project Management Necessary?

If it's implemented correctly then agile project management can benefit every project manager out there to some degree. To first understand why this is the case, let's take a closer look at what agile project management is.

Agile project management is a less restrictive approach to project management. It caters for a far more interactive and flexible process. Whilst this seems to initially go against the tradition of being organized, working to set timeframes and within set parameters, there are instances when it is essential.

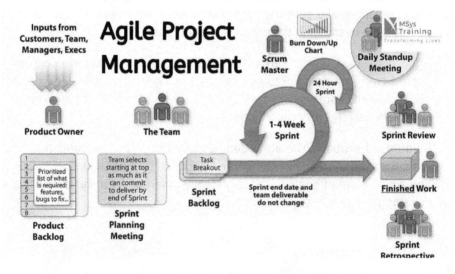

It is most often used in projects that require the development of software. It is the most effective form of project management for any project that includes high levels of change and risk over a short period of time.

This approach does also bring a new set of challenges to the table. With flexibility comes an increased chance of things going awry. In order to combat this we must ensure the foundations of the team are built around honesty, excellent communication, and discipline. These attributes correctly implemented will ensure the whole team stays focused and keeps moving in the correct direction, even through periods of change.

The true key to success in project management is balance. It means knowing not just the correct practices to implement, but also the correct importance and time that should be spent on each one. There are aspects of agile project management that will impact any project in a positive manner.

The increased focus on team management and group accountability always leads to a happier more productive team. A happier team leads to a more productive team, which is never a bad thing.

The ability to adapt builds creativity and innovation at the ground level. This means problem solving and potential obstacles are dealt with much more efficiently.

The increased interaction with customers allows the team to gain a better understanding and consistently deliver more reliable results. Planning for the unknown is an essential ingredient of agile project management. Creating contingencies for problems can't be a bad thing.

Build a team to suit your approach

When you are planning for a project with attributes suggesting agile PM is the best way to proceed, then building your team with the approach in mind can greatly increase the ease with which you work.

The ideal team will be energetic, innovative, and welcoming of change. Include all team members at every stage of planning, allowing you to ensure the deadlines can be met, and highlighting any potential problems that may need contingencies creating.

Once the project is underway ensure you're in constant contact with all key team members. Making yourself available will minimize the time needed to solve problems and answer questions, and maximize the effects of good communication and teamwork.

As you become more comfortable with agile projects, maybe by attending an agile PM training course, you will start to see the way in which it can be used to benefit most projects.

Chapter 25

Tips For Making Agile Less Fragile

In some shops, agile means extremely small sprints that are continuously deployed, sometimes multiple times per day. For others, it means the same old waterfall-style development, but they have burndown charts, daily stand-up meetings, and maybe someone with the title of "SCRUM Master." Regardless of how teams define agile, their common goal is increased velocity meaning faster product delivery and better ROI.

Purely agile teams and barely agile teams have something else in common: They forget to consider agile support.

Agile development and agile support go hand-in-hand. Agile development can only save you so much time if you're wasting time on the backend trying to pinpoint errors and correct them. I don't know any developers who look forward to rework.

And they don't exactly look forward to going to IT with their problems because IT doesn't want to hear them. IT is busy. That means, you have to do more application support in addition to everything else you're already doing in the same number of hours.

As you well know, building great software means more than just creating cool or useful features. Users want a great experience. And yet there you are: You're developing code and hopefully releasing it often but your shrinking development cycle may not account for the proper level of load, acceptance and other testing because management thinks you should spend all of your time coding.

But because you know software has to be properly tested, you hope and pray your application will behave well in production after launch. Sometimes it does, sometimes it doesn't. Sometimes it works for a while and then fails at an inconvenient time. When your application fails, you have to find out what went wrong, quickly.

Agile support is similar to agile development in that it requires a simple plan for quick execution and accomplishing goals. When you make agile support a part agile development, you can achieve higher levels of quality and get to market faster than ever before if you do it right. I recommend three things:

1: Plan for Support

You already know your application is going to fail at some point and that your development team is going to have to respond. But have you actually included support as part of your development plan? Probably not because as I mentioned earlier management thinks you should be spending all of your time coding.

At the same time, the very same managers demand continuous productivity and efficiency improvements. If you simply tell them that support is a bottleneck, they may not believe you. But when a major outage occurs, the bottleneck becomes obvious. You know. You've been there before.

If you include agile support as part of your plan from the beginning, support will seem a lot less chaotic later.

2: Don't Over-Architect or Under-Architect

Anyone familiar with agile development understands the concept of breaking a project into smaller pieces. In practice, when your project has become a collection of agile pieces, it may be difficult to see the whole and therefore difficult to build a large architecture that will scale and work with the end product.

Many times, a SCRUM master or project manager will take the time to plan The World's Greatest Application Architecture full of logging, well-calculated scalability and a high focus on easy maintainability.

But, because neither project deadlines nor budget requirements are infinite, The World's Greatest Application Architecture ends up being little more than a pipe dream because at the end of the day, unless you are writing and selling software toolkits, business stakeholders don't really care about software architecture. They care about features that sell.

Even if you did build The World's Greatest Application Architecture, you'd probably discover too late that you've over-built some aspect of your application that will take far too long to refactor. What's important in architecting your application is that you:

Don't do dumb things. If you're doing agile development, you're working in small increments and should have good visibility into the code that's being produced. You should also think about how your code will scale and perform.

Achieve consistency. Try to use consistent logging, error handling, and configuration management. In code reviews, make sure you adhere to these standards. If each developer has decided to handle errors and logging in a different way, supporting your application becomes a nightmare.

Don't allow unhandled exceptions to be caught and thrown away, for example. For most programming languages, there are tools available that can help enforce some of these basic rules.

Document. While you don't need to detail every aspect of your application, you should include things done in the spirit of "get it to ship" that will cause pain in the future. Go ahead and add a backlog item for it, and try to prioritize it as soon as possible. After all, if you plan time for it, you should be able to improve it in an upcoming sprint.

Don't reinvent the wheel. We all know "that developer" who will spend a lifetime crafting a better way to parse a Boolean value or do other things that allow The Daily WTF to exist. Don't let it happen. If someone has already built a great framework or SDK that will help expedite your product's architecture, embrace it.

3: Have a Disaster Plan

Even if you haven't done what I suggest in points #1 and #2 (Plan for Support and Don't Over-Architect or Under-Architect), you should know what to do when things go south. This is where I often see developers hiding under their desks curled in a fetal position and begging for their mommies. Things have gone to hell, the boss is furious, and the phone won't stop ringing.

Isolating and solving production issues is always a bit tricky, but isn't that big of a deal if you at least think about how you're going to handle it. You need a "go bag" and I'm going to help you build it. Here's what you need:

Be ready to reproduce. So often, I see developers who don't know how to troubleshoot a bug. Sometimes it just comes down to common sense: Get the steps to reproduce and use some basic tools to observe and troubleshoot the issue.

You'd be amazed how many times my query, "have you used an HTTP proxy tool to inspect the results of the request" is met with a blank stare from the developer who is assigned to an Urgent production bug. I feel this aspect of development is often overlooked, and needs to be exercised often, just like any muscle.

Know where to find your apps. Your production environment shouldn't be a complete mystery. You should know how many instances of your app are out there and how to access them. Ideally, you should also have a way to isolate the issue to a particular instance if at all possible.

In some environments, none of this is available to developers. You should at least know who holds the keys, and be prepared to establish a good line of communication, or invest in a product that allow safe, secure access.

Know how to get your data. As mentioned in Tip # 2 (Don't Over-Architect, Don't Under-Architect), you should at least decide on some consistent logging and error handling. Maybe you don't have access, but you should be able to tell your support/operations team exactly where to get all the data you need to troubleshoot and analyze the issue.

Have access to the right tools. You will eventually find an issue that can't be resolved through simple reproduction, logging, and error handling. It will be a sporadic issue that seems to have no pattern or occurs completely unexpectedly and "resolves itself" just as quickly.

When that happens, you need the tools available and at hand to perform a much more detailed analysis which may include advanced application health monitoring, code profiling, SQL profiling, failed request tracing, or memory/crash/process dumps.

Regardless of platform, there are tools out there to do all of these things, and you need to have them ready and at your disposal. Work with your Operations team to make sure they are installed and, if possible, configured to capture data automatically under certain conditions.

Bottom Line:

No one likes to plan for failures, but they're inevitable. That's why you have to sit through a short safety lecture before every commercial airline flight and why FEMA exists. With some simple planning, you will be able to easily support your application when disaster strikes and come out looking like a hero.

Chapter 26

Adopting Agile Development Methodology To Achieve Success

The ever-changing nature of the world's economy has created a dire need for companies to be ever on dynamic front. This has resulted in companies throughout the world to invest their considerable amount of money and time in adopting new and different methodologies, tools and technologies.

It is imperative today to be forever ready to adapt and practice latest software development methodologies. Adopting the latest technologies is the only solution to survive in this cutthroat competition. And, one such latest methodology is agile development methodology.

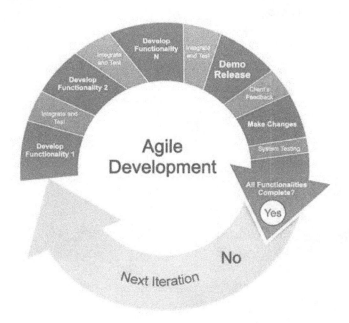

Though agile is not a new methodology- as some agilists admit that it has been in practice since decades. Yet it is very lately that this approach has witnessed a dramatic surge in its practice worldwide, owing to changing economies. Traditional agilists also believe that this methodology is an umbrella term for a set of fundamental principles to develop a software by emphasizing more on human and product interaction.

Agile methodology is an approach that applies collaborative and continuous improvement concepts to develop softwares. In this approach, flexible business processes are developed agile, so that a company can quickly develop mass customized products at a mass-production speed and efficiency.

Owing to this, the company can also rapidly introduce a steady succession of latest products in the market. During agile methodology, a company encounters new concepts, new methods, and new roles, principally everything in a new way. It lets a company cope up with fast changing markets, ever-changing product requirements and complex problems.

In broader terms, agile methodology means to create processes that are unique and flexible in making products in order to respond quickly to the changing market conditions.

Agile software development also creates better working relationships among all the team members, increases collective responsibility and keeps project focused on customer and market needs.

In particular, agile method offers a working framework where functional and technical func6tions keep on evolving, thus, maintain a focus on rapid delivery of ROI.

Agile development methodology also accelerates the delivery of initial business value through optimized development process. It also ensures that accurate visibility is available throughout a project, thus, at the end of the project, agile product development boosts the business by addressing customer needs.

In a nutshell, agile methodology concentrates highly on:

1) Individuals and interactions- over processes and tools

2) Working software- over documentation

3) Customer collaboration- over negotiation

4) Responding to change- over following a operational plan

Unlike its predecessor, the waterfall model, Agile is highly dependent on the initial specifications and the view of the final product. Agile is all about agility. Agile software development methods are considered as high revenue boosters for product companies looking to bring great products to market in time.

Let's take a look at the top 10 key advantages of agile development-

1. Time to Market

Leading ISVs go to market earlier than their competitors, giving themselves an edge over competitors. If an ISV wants to position themselves at the very helm of their industry, the best way would be to get to market early with their product. Agile development's key methodology of evolution through collaboration improves the time to market by a great extent.

2. Flexibility

In other software development models, the ability to make modifications to the initial specification may be quite hard due to their inherent nature. In case of agile development, flexibility is a major aspect that allows project managers and the clients to modify after the initial planning.

3. High Level of Engagement

Agile methodology allows the client's team and the product development vendor's team to operate as one integrated team, wherein the responsibilities are well defined and modification requests are readily available. High degree of collaboration is the major reason why agile is a success.

4. High Quality

Quality assurance engineering is a major aspect of software development. Ensuring high quality in software is possible only by integrating the QA team with the development team. This principle is integrated in the agile development methodology. And QA personnel are able to do regular inspections of the project as it develops.

5. Transparency

Active involvement of the development, operations, and quality teams makes the agile methodology quite transparent. Stakeholders need in-depth visibility into the various aspects of the project, which is ensured in agile methodology.

6. Delivery Management

Management of deliverables is smooth and straightforward in case of agile development. Also, the delivery timeline stays so predictable that both you and the vendor can fix your schedules accordingly and plan other relevant activities such as marketing.

7. Cost-Effectiveness

Predictability on the schedule of release and collaborative effort have a major effect on the cost of the product. Fixing the budget and controlling it well can make the product highly cost-effective. No other software development model provides better cost-effectiveness than the agile model.

8. Client Satisfaction

Agile model goes through software sprints involving verification and validation phases. This is highly integrated with the user requirement specifications, functional and design specifications, code review, testing, etc.

As a result, the client has ample time to review the progress and provide necessary feedback for improvement. At the end of the day, this creates a high level of satisfaction for your client, and further the customers of the product.

9. Better Management of Risks

Agile methodology is characterized by incremental releases that provide opportunity to manage unforeseen risks. For a software product company, identifying risks at the early stages makes all the difference.

10. Keep Up With the Industry Changes

With agile methodology, you are able to keep up with the changes that happen in the industry. Each sprint of the model gives a full-fledged model as well as ample opportunity to modify the specifications for the next release.

Adding and removing features, hence, is pretty easy within the agile model. This allows you to keep up with the changes happening in the industry, a key reason why the agile model is called that.

Other software development methodologies, such as the waterfall model, incremental development, iterative development, etc., have their advantages and disadvantages. But when we look at the business in a marketing perspective, then agile methodology may be the right model.

Conclusion

With the changing market dynamics, emergence of advanced technologies, ever-changing customer preferences, and evolving global standards and compliance requirements, agile development practices are moving into the mainstream.

Today, most application development teams are in the process of shifting to agile methods to do more iterative development. Shifting to agile practices is a challenging task, and it requires extreme focus towards quality and improved collaboration. Most enterprises often fail to implement agile appropriately, and this forms the main reason for agile projects failing to deliver high quality software.

Though many organizations aim to implement Agile, most of them still tend to schedule all their testing activities towards the end of SDLC and undertake testing as a distinct activity rather than as an overall agile process.

Typically, most agile development projects just run as traditional waterfall model where the developer works on the requirements and hands over the developed software to the QA team for testing.

In few instances where testing moves along with development, most QA activities are performed by members of the team who are also involved in designing or development of the project. These kinds of approaches contradict the fundamental concepts of agile development.

Pure agile practices focus on ensuring the quality from a user's perspective and this requires testing to be involved right from establishing the scope of the project.

Though daily meetings have become a part of the agile process, testing is yet to become a natural part of the entire agile project and not any phase after coding has been done.

Greater emphasis must be laid on building up quality right from the ground up to protect many problems that might arise down the line.

Developers and testers should work along to bring down the requirements and design problems as early as possible in the software life cycle.

While continuous integration is the core of the agile project, continuous testing will help enterprises to reduce the risk involved in the project and ultimately deliver high-quality software. It is also critical for organizations to ensure strong collaboration among all involved in the agile project.

 Requirements change as we get deeper into the software life cycle and quality goals become a moving target. Strong collaboration will help address the changes in requirements and design. Overall, continuous testing with quick feedback loop, use of latest automation tools, expertise agile testers, strong collaboration and quality responsibility among all involved will determine the success of an agile project.

For many companies still using the waterfall method and other older forms of software development, new methodologies, such agile development, present opportunities to create new products more quickly and in line with consumer demand.

However, before an organization adopts agile development software and methods, it should asses their structure and goals to be sure that it is the right fit. Wasting time and money on failed implementations can be devastating for organizations hoping to compete in the modern software industry.

For organizations planning to offer hosted software, agile makes the most sense for a number of reasons. Firstly, since customers do not have to install anything, it's easy to implement any updates that come along with new iterations.

With more enterprise IT departments and decision-makers hoping to implement hosted software and other forms of cloud computing, faster product development that still factors accountability and effectiveness into the process is crucial.

When implementing agile development or any new process, change management is an important aspect of the move. If, in the past, a company struggled to adapt when altering a system, making adjustments to this process is crucial to the success of the agile development initiative. However, the successful deployment of agile practices has helped organizations provide customers with stronger, easier-to-use products

Finally, if you enjoyed this book, then I'd like to ask you for a favor, would you be kind enough to leave a review for this book on Amazon? It'd be greatly appreciated!

Leave a review for this book on Amazon!

www.ingramcontent.com/pod-product-compliance
Lightning Source LLC
Chambersburg PA
CBHW071223050326

40689CB00011B/2425